Bound by Love

Bound by Love

The journey of Lily Nie and thousands
of China's forsaken children

by Linda Droeger

Chinese Children Charities Publishing

Chinese Children Charities Publishing
6920 South Holly Circle
Centennial, Colorado 80112

Editor: Brian Schoeni
Cover illustration: Mary GrandPré
Calligraphy: Nie Guang Qian

Library of Congress Cataloging-in-Publication Data

Droeger, Linda.
  Bound by love : the journey of Lily Nie and thousands of China's forsaken children / by Linda Droeger. -- 1st ed.
    p. cm.
  ISBN 978-0-615-34737-0
  1. Abandoned children--China. 2. Orphans--China. 3. Intercountry adoption--China. I. Title.

HV847.C6D76 2010
362.76092--dc22
[B]

                              2010001352

3   15

For the children, whose struggles and strength inspire.

For the families and their tears of joy and sorrow.

For the countless people, East and West,
who cared enough to change fate.

For China, who shared her children
and built a bridge that will forever connect
our cultures and our families.

(Chinese character for *love*)

Contents

Points of interest in "Bound by Love"

Fu nu neng ding ban bian tian.

Women hold up half the sky.

PROLOGUE
1962

The nurse searched the young woman's unflinching eyes. There was no anger in them, nor fear. All she could see was determination. "I need an abortion," the woman said again. "I am not leaving."

For three days this woman had refused to leave the army hospital, insisting that the doctors terminate her pregnancy. Three days without drama, only a calm persistence that she was wise enough to know her own world, and it did not have room for another life.

It was the end of China's Great Famine. Thirty million people had died of starvation in the world's worst food shortage. Before that, the young woman had survived the battlefields of two brutal wars, the first in China, the second in Korea.

"Do you have any children?" the nurse demanded.

"Yes. One," she answered. "A girl."

She thought of her seven-year-old daughter, living day and night in a child-care center, while her parents worked round the clock.

"One is not enough," the nurse declared. "You should have another. Perhaps you'll be blessed with a boy."

The nurse's gaze sharpened. Something had passed over the young woman's face like the shadow a diving hawk casts on the ground, too fast for the conscious mind to truly comprehend, but a flicker of some unforeseen strength.

"I need an abortion."

The nurse could not know what that fleeting shadow signified. How could she?

Liu Liang Zhen knew she did not need to justify herself. She had seen too much, done too much, to believe this was an issue of gender.

Perhaps you'll have a boy.

No. She already knew the strength a woman could possess. She heard Chairman Mao's thundering voice, resonating deep inside her.

Fu nu neng ding ban bian tian!
Women hold up half the sky!

This was about survival. This was about a future carved in stone rather than scratched into the muddy road as a throng of clattering bicycles crashed forward like the tide.

I want an abortion.

Two days later, Liang Zhen fought back tears, scolding herself. How could she, a member of the victorious People's Liberation Army, admit defeat? She knew thousands of others before her had received the abortions they sought. What had made the hospital staff say no to her? Perhaps it was something she could not see.

Regardless, as she set her eyes forward she knew that her family was about to undergo a shift. They would no longer be just three.

On July 12, 1963, in the city of Yingkou in the far northeastern province of Liaoning, her child was born — a girl. She must have absorbed some of her mother's iron strength, and her father sensed it. For her name, he chose Li Li — stands up straight and independent.

Qi er bu she.

Never give up.

ONE

ACROSS THE FROZEN RIVER
1984 – 1985

Nie Li Li pedaled steadily away from the University of Fushun toward the old stone bridge that stretched over the Hun River, whose strong current flowed silently under a thick layer of winter ice. Sitting tall on her shiny bicycle, Li Li's long, black hair flowed from beneath her fur hat and intertwined with the tails of her woolen scarf, billowing in the bitter wind.

On this afternoon, she navigated home, swept along in a stream of cyclists jingling their bells as they jockeyed for passage among the horse-drawn wagons, beeping buses, and pedicabs that flowed down the unpaved streets of Fushun.

Bent into the wind, many of the solemn cyclists grimaced as they ground forward. But Li Li's face was glowing. At twenty-one, riding a bike still felt to her like flying. It gave her a taste of independence in a life bound by family expectations and the iron grip of communism. Her bicycle, her most prized possession, allowed her the freedom to leave home whenever she wished, although she obeyed the warnings of her mother, Liu Liang Zhen, not to stop along the streets. As a young singer and dancer in Mao Zedong's communist army, Liang Zhen had learned to ignore soldiers who called out to pretty women. She had taught Li Li the same lesson as a school girl growing up during the Cultural Revolution when marauding young Red Guards brought violence to the streets: Keep moving forward.

Ahead at the bridge, a thin, young man restlessly pushed up the sleeve of his coat and checked his watch again. For more than two hours he'd waited. The late afternoon light was slowly fading, and the cold, hard ground he squatted on was said in Fushun to be frozen three feet deep. He shifted his weight, relieving the pressure on his back from the steel frame of his old-fashioned bike.

As he watched the parade of students pedaling home, he realized the colleague he'd begged to substitute for him had by now dismissed the English class he was supposed to teach. He felt no regret. The chance to see her was far more powerful than the risk of losing his teaching position at the local college in a town to which he'd never wanted to return.

Behind the glasses that covered much of his face, he squinted, searching the crowded street for a glimpse of the face of the graceful young woman he was looking for.

There was a saying often used to describe Fushun, the coal capital of China:

Mei pi pu di. Ma fen suo bian. Qi che yi pao yi liu yan.

The land is covered by coal. The streets are lined with horse manure. The passing vehicles stir up the dust.

Ever since he could remember, he badly wanted to escape this filthy city where he was born. His father, who grew up herding pigs as the son of a poor rice farmer, called him Hui. It was a name the young man first changed to the English name Brook, because he liked the romance of it. Then he changed it to Wallace, which could be translated to Chinese to mean "gentleman from China." Finally, he changed it to Joshua, from a book strictly forbidden in his homeland.

When at last he spotted her striking figure in the dull sea of black and blue, he was astonished once again by her beauty in this place of ugliness. He leapt to his feet, whisking up his bike. Boldly, he breezed up beside her.

When she saw him her hands reflexively hit the brakes, wobbling her bike. In an instant, she regained control.

"You ride home this way?" he asked cheerfully.

He thought back to the first time he saw her. Between classes at the university, he was climbing up the stairs, talking to the student chairman of the Economic Reform Club when he had stopped midsentence.

The club chairman looked around and quickly saw what riveted Joshua. He stepped in and filled the silence.

"This is Mr. Zhong, our new English teacher," he said. "And this is Nie Li Li, a law student."

In that moment, her brilliance seemed to illuminate the dimness of the stairwell. One look at her face told the English teacher that this woman's family came from southern China, famous for its lovely women. The smooth skin of her oval face was nothing like the rough, broad faces of the women of the northeast. The unusual beauty of her face she had inherited from her mother, the daughter of a Guangxi Supreme Court justice. Her large, double-lidded eyes came from her father, the son of an entrepreneur who made and lost a fortune before becoming a government official.

By Chinese standards, double lids made a woman's eyes exquisite. All her life she had been told by friends that her eyes were her best feature. Even though her eyesight was poor, she kept her glasses hidden in her pocket at school, shyly retrieving them only when she needed to read the blackboard.

Not only was the English teacher dazzled by her beauty, he was struck by her stature. At five foot six inches, the slender woman was taller than most Chinese women — and many men. Her regal carriage, the result of being drilled by her army parents to stand erect and dignified, made her seem unattainable. In that first moment, somewhere deep inside, he vowed to marry her, even though she showed not a trace of interest in him.

What Li Li first noticed about the English teacher was his height. He was short, barely taller than she was. His hair seemed stripped of its deep black color, like the faded hair of the Chinese who had grown up without enough to eat. He wore it long, combed over to one side. He was twenty-two, but the crow's feet etched into the corners of his eyes made him look older. Dressed in a Western-cut suit and narrow tie, he looked nothing like the young men enrolled at the university who mostly wore traditional Mao suits.

Now, after the surprise of seeing him at the bridge, Li Li's calm resolve returned.

"I have to get going home," she said.

"I'll ride with you," he said happily.

She did not protest, although inside she felt annoyed; his status as a teacher was something she could not ignore. Li Li was sought by many young men in school, but she resisted the advances of them all. She wondered what her parents would think of this stranger in a suit and tie if he insisted on seeing her to the door.

Riding alongside her, he noticed that her bike was sparkling clean. His was covered in a heavy layer of black soot.

In this industrial city in 1984, everywhere were reminders that coal was still king. A statue of Chairman Mao stood on the spot where the communist dictator once rallied local coal miners. It was during his disastrous Great Leap Forward in the late 1950s that the revered but ruthless ruler arrived in Fushun to urge the miners to work faster to fuel the industrial juggernaut he was masterminding. His plan was to make China a world power by reigniting the country's ravaged economy on the backs of people like Joshua's parents, who worked day and night in the coal-fired factories.

Li Li's parents, who had marched in the triumphant People's Liberation Army that ushered communism into China in 1949, moved to Fushun when Li Li was three. She was still a small girl when her father took her to see the city's most famous spectacle, an open coal mine four miles across and a thousand feet deep. She had expected coal to come from a cave carved deep underground. But a tiny trickle of water that began its inexorable journey thousands of years ago had steadily sliced a grand canyon through the rock, exposing shiny black coal around pools of shimmering water. What nature had revealed became the largest open mine in all of China. Seeing it made her understand the name people had given the famous mine:

Lu tian.
Everything up under the sky.

The mine changed everything under the sky in Fushun, countless lives of miners and factory workers over generations past and for generations to come. It was the smokestacks towering over the factories, spewing yellow-gray smoke and black soot that made everything dirty.

"How do you keep your bike so clean?" the inquisitive English teacher asked.

Like other students, her bicycle was covered in a layer of soot every morning when she arrived at the university. But by day's end, one of her secret admirers had polished it clean.

Li Li shrugged, glancing wistfully at the shop where she normally stopped to buy *nai dou,* the milk beans she snacked on during the long ride home from law school.

Her family's apartment was a thirty-minute bike ride from the college, but that did not stop young men from following her home. When they asked if she had a boyfriend, she did not hesitate. "Yes," she answered, even though it was a lie. Her parents had taught her to tell the truth, but this deception was necessary.

It was nearly dark when they parked their bicycles in front of the apartment building where Li Li's family lived.

"I'll carry your bike up," he said.

"I can get it," she insisted.

But he had already hoisted the bicycle up on his shoulder, smiling. "I've got it."

Seeing he would not take no for an answer, she allowed him to lead her up the stairs to the fourth floor.

At the door, her mother greeted them warmly. She was glad to invite her second daughter's friends into her home, especially on the rare occasions that Li Li brought a young man with her. Unlike other Chinese women, Liang Zhen had never been concerned about bearing a son, but it was no secret that she wanted her youngest daughter to marry, as her oldest daughter had. If a young woman in China did not find a suitable husband while in her twenties, her parents would arrange a marriage to spare her the shame of being single.

Joshua's eyes swept across the spacious government apartment provided to families of former army officers. Never had this young man known anyone who lived in a three-bedroom apartment — with its own bathroom, no less. His gut tightened as he mentally compared the home his family of six grew up in — one room, less than one hundred and fifty square feet in size — and thought of the public restrooms his family shared with neighbors. Something in his soul stirred, and he longed for a better life, one that he could not afford.

Closing his book, Li Li's father, a government worker, rose from his chair. At nearly six feet, he towered over Joshua.

"What are you studying at the university?" Nie Guang Qian asked.

"I teach English."

"English?" Li Li's father said, surprised. "Where did you go to college?"

Joshua wished his answer could have been different.

"Dalian Foreign Language Institute."

Dalian was respected, but it was not the university that the young man so driven to learn English had set his sights on.

His obsession to learn the language of Westerners had taken root as a boy in a neighborhood movie house. The ten-year-old had lined up with other children to see Mao's latest newsreel. Inside the packed theater, the boy was mesmerized by the communist ruler's first meeting with the president of the United States. But what impressed him most about Richard Nixon's historic visit in 1972 was the translator at Mao's side. To Joshua, the message was clear. The way to earn a place next to the most powerful leaders in the world was to speak English. He spent the next decade determined to learn it.

In a twist of fate, it was his knowledge of English that helped doom his dream to go to a prestigious university and escape Fushun forever. His heart was set on Nankai University, the alma mater of Premier Chou Enlai, the leader instrumental in the Communist Party's meteoric rise to power. Joshua had the second-best score among more than 20,000 graduating high school students in the first national college entrance examination in Fushun, and he seemed assured of a place at Nankai. It was a shock when the government informed him that his academic records had been lost. Instead of an acceptance letter to Nankai, he received an order to go to Dalian. Crushed, he had no choice but to obey. The final blow came when he graduated from the foreign language institute and was forced back to his hometown to teach English.

"Where do your parents work?" Li Li's father asked, trying to measure the young man his daughter had brought into his home.

"In the shoe factory," Joshua answered in a determinedly steady voice.

What Joshua didn't tell him was that his mother never learned to read or write, and his father had to drop out of school in the eighth grade to help his family with farm work. Joshua had a quick mind like his parents, who were bright but born into poor families that had little opportunity to educate their children. They worked hard to get ahead in the shoe factory, where his mother rose from entry Level One to Level Seven, and his father achieved the top ranking of Level Eight.

Li Li's father, an army colonel turned government writer and historian, and her mother, an accountant, placed the highest value on education. Li Li was not yet in school when her parents first discovered her academic gifts. Her mother read her the Tang Dynasty poems she loved, and Li Li began parroting back the verses word for word. One day when her father returned from work, the tiny girl stood before him and recited her first poem. The praise from her tall, imposing *baba* delighted her. Her keen memory came from her father, whose power of recollection was extraordinary. He had memorized many poems from the Tang and Song dynasties, most of the teachings of Confucius, and long sections of the books he devoured. Each day when her mother finished work, she helped Li Li memorize a new poem to present to her *baba*. By seven, she could recite well over a hundred.

Joshua's family had no time and no money for books that his mother could not read. His earliest memories were of worrying about getting enough to eat. While Li Li's parents brought home plenty of rice, meat, vegetables, and fruits from the army cafeteria, Joshua's mother spent hours waiting in line for the family's meager food rations. The boy longed for some rice to eat, but most days there was none in the house. The only vegetables were the salty turnips his family dried on their roof. Because Mao was shipping the abundant local coal to stoke southern industry, fuel was also scarce during the cold winters. Li Li's family kept warm in their heated army apartment building. On the other side of the icy Hun River, Joshua's family chipped bark from tree trunks to burn under their mud-and-grass brick *kang,* the traditional Chinese family bed where all six of them slept.

The only thing the two families had in common was that the heads of both had endured the cruel persecution of relentless interrogators during Mao's Cultural Revolution. Joshua's father, a working-class "Red," was the victim of false accusations at the shoe factory. Li Li's father, labeled a "Black," was accused by the army of being the son of a landlord, the enemy of the communists.

It came as no surprise to the English teacher that Li Li's father would look down on a suitor from a poor, uneducated family. Joshua knew a match was entirely improbable.

The Economic Reform Club became a way for Joshua to see Li Li. She had recently joined the club, stirred by the appeal of Mao's successor, President Deng Xiaoping, for young people to create their own economic opportunities in ways impossible in their parents' generation. Mao's death in 1976 had loosened communism's repressive hold, and students were rallying to the call to transform China into an entrepreneurial economy. For the first time in decades, young people had a sense of their own mastership, a hope to one day open their own businesses.

At a club gathering one evening, the English teacher offered to ride home with Li Li on the bus. Out of respect, she allowed him to escort her, even though she was worried what people would think. Dating among students was strictly forbidden at the university, and the idea of a teacher dating a student was unfathomable. Government officials who caught students in romantic relationships broke them up, ordering couples to move to different parts of the country. After all, the government paid for students to go to school, and they were expected to devote their whole minds — and hearts — to their studies.

Joshua constantly schemed to see her, but Li Li was focused on her last few months of law school and her girlfriends. Late into the evenings, friends would jam into her bedroom to listen to the latest hit songs. Her love of music she learned from her mother, who as a girl learned to play eight different instruments. Li Li played violin and guitar, and she loved to listen to the Singapore singers' popular songs on her prized cassette recorder, which was wired to a set of speakers.

During the Cultural Revolution, which lasted until the mid-1970s, the Chinese sought to acquire the Big Three: a bicycle, a radio, and a watch. By the early 1980s when Li Li was in college, that shifted to a refrigerator, a TV, and a cassette player. Li Li's father was fascinated by modern technology, and her family was the first in the neighborhood to get all three. Her sister, Ke Ke, worked on an assembly line in an electronics factory, earning four dollars a month to build TVs. Ke Ke was able to snag a set of speakers from the factory for her little sister at a deep discount. None of Li Li's friends had a way for the friends to listen to music together, much less a bedroom of their own. It put Li Li in a position of envy.

As the months passed, whenever Joshua could convince someone to substitute for him, he dashed away from class to try to catch Li Li at the bridge. Many times it was dark when he gave up waiting and pedaled his bike home alone. Again and again he returned to the bridge until eventually he met up with her. On those happy afternoons, he rode home with her, lingering at the door long enough for her gracious mother to invite him in.

Li Li remained reserved, but Joshua was perfectly comfortable doing all the talking. As he grew to know her, he learned that they both had attended the same high school at the same time. Even though Joshua was a year ahead of her, he wondered how it was that he'd never noticed her. It was one of the few things they had in common, and he searched for other ways to bridge the vast gap between them.

Li Li could not help but find the lively English teacher more interesting than the other young university men whose conversation was limited to the mundane events of ordinary days. Joshua regaled her with stories of his days in Dalian as a student tour guide, escorting fashionable Westerners about the sophisticated seaside town on the Yellow Sea that was fast becoming the Hong Kong of the Northeast. Despite her seemingly cool reaction, his tales stirred in her a desire for the adventure that eluded her in the sheltered life she lived under her parents' roof.

The English teacher was quick-witted, and when he joked with her she sometimes dropped her guard and laughed out loud. Not many boys could make her laugh the way he did. Still, as the day of her law-school graduation grew closer, Li Li did nothing to encourage Joshua's advances — but neither did she discourage them. In the Nie home, under the critical eye of her father, Li Li for the first time allowed herself to be wooed, even though it unnerved her.

In China in the late twentieth century, a young man dared not declare his love outright to a woman. It simply wasn't done. But on April 6, 1985, Joshua found a way to tell Li Li. She returned home late one evening to find him waiting for her. In his hands he held a package.

"Open it," he said, handing it to her.

Slowly she unfolded the paper. Inside was Chinese calligraphy, an art form requiring years of practice to master. In Joshua's graceful Chinese characters was his personal pledge to the woman he'd fallen in love with:

> *Qi er bu she.*
> Never give up.

"You're serious," she said, staring into his solemn face.

"I will never leave you."

His words slowly penetrated, sinking beneath her calm surface into the swirling depths. She stood and carried the calligraphy into her bedroom, and together they hung it above the door.

For the first time, it fully sunk in. This man she'd allowed to court her would pursue her until she said yes, no matter how long it took. It was as if something that had stood between them suddenly shifted, as if she'd been watching him from afar, and now, inexplicably, a door into her heart cracked open. She now saw him not as just another suitor, but as a man who could one day become her husband.

Still, she had no idea if she would let him.

Attorney Nie straightened the collar on her neatly ironed blouse and brushed the street dust from the blue business suit provided by her employer, Fushun Law Firm II, where her monthly salary as a beginning lawyer was seven dollars. In impoverished China, it was enough to put her in the upper class.

At her desk she read through the contract she had prepared for a business client. On the lapel of her jacket was a badge officially identifying her as an attorney, one of the first students to pass the bar examination since the universities reopened more than a decade after Mao shut them down in the Cultural Revolution. It stood as a mark of pride, but also as a silent reminder that law was not her mother's first choice for her.

Her mother's dream had been for her high-achieving daughter to become a healer like Liang Zhen's father, a judge better known by his neighbors for his herbal medicine miracles. Li Li still could not shake the painful memory of the day she told her mother that she'd failed the science college entrance test in math, physics, and chemistry. The grueling annual examination was Li Li's gateway to studying medicine — the gateway to bringing her parents' dreams to fruition.

A student's entire future rode on the outcome of the entrance exam. Millions of China's high school graduates took the three-day test in either the social sciences or hard sciences. Only two or three percent passed, but Li Li was at the top of her class and everyone expected her to excel. To fail the college entrance exam was considered so disastrous to Chinese families that some students committed suicide rather than face their parents.

Gathering her strength but feeling smaller than ever, Li Li had taken a deep breath.

"Mama, I failed the exam."

Stirring a pot as she prepared dinner, her mother gasped and whirled around to face her. "What happened?" she demanded, shocked.

"I don't know," Li Li said, lowering her eyes.

Turning away so her mother would not see the tears welling in her eyes, Li Li walked outside on to the balcony where her father's hot pepper plants grew and gazed at Fushun's glum smokestacks belching soot into the air. Humiliation burned in her chest.

She knew that flunking the exam would be devastating to her parents. Their daughter's failure meant that they would lose face. Disappointing them was far worse than losing the chance to attend medical school. Never again, she vowed silently, would she allow herself to fail.

The following year she passed the social sciences test in literature, history, and geography. Her acceptance into the University of Fushun's law department seemed to satisfy her mother, who had drilled into Li Li since childhood that girls were not only as good as boys, but more capable.

Now Li Li was a professional lawyer, and on this day in 1985 she was meeting some law associates. After their business was complete, she was walking back to the office along the bustling streets of Fushun. Pulled from her thoughts, she spotted a sign she had never before noticed.

Fushun She Hui Fu Li Yuan
Fushun Social Welfare Institute

In the barren yard, young school-age girls were playing, their faces dirty and their clothes tattered. She had never paid much attention to children, but that day it was as if there was an undertow, drawing her inside. It wasn't a school, so what were these children doing here?

A worker stopped her. Li Li pointed to her attorney's badge, and the woman motioned her in. Li Li slowly walked down the hall and poked her head inside a room. By the pillows and folded blankets at each end of the bed, she could see that the children slept two to a bed.

She turned back into the hall and tracked down a caretaker.

"Why are they here?" Li Li asked her.

The caretaker stared back. "They have no home."

Seven years had passed since China had implemented its rigid One-Child Policy, restricting families from having more than one baby. It was the government's desperate effort to control the nation's wildly spiraling population, which had topped one billion — one-fifth of the world's population. Mao's fear of invaders had once helped fuel the rapid growth, as he urged parents to have huge families in order to protect the nation. The Chinese loved their children, but after the One-Child Policy, women were under tremendous pressure from husbands and in-laws to produce a male child to carry on the family name and to fulfill the centuries-old tradition that sons care for their aging parents.

Like most Chinese, Li Li had no idea that the One-Child Policy had resulted in the abandonment of thousands of newborn girls, sometimes without their mothers' consent, so families could try again to birth a boy. The babies were left in cardboard boxes, baskets, and rice sacks along the side of the road, amid vegetables and fruits at street markets, or on the steps of police stations and government buildings. Sometimes a baby was alone in the cold for hours until some stranger found the child and delivered her to the local orphanage.

In that moment, the secret life of China's abandoned babies washed over her, unsettling the calm, predictable flow of her accomplished life. Li Li had witnessed a harsh reality the world, not to mention most of China, was oblivious to.

⁓

Only a few months after her first day at Fushun Law Firm II, Li Li was given the plum assignment of traveling up and down China's east coast as far north as Harbin and south to Changsha to negotiate business contracts and take companies to court when they failed to live up to their agreements.

As the year passed, she spent more than half her time traveling away from home. Joshua's courtship shifted from charming her with conversation to wooing her in the pages of the love letters he faithfully wrote to her each day. He chose his words carefully, writing and rewriting, hoping that his letters would serve to bind them together, even though he knew that most of the time he was far from her mind.

Always when Li Li returned to Fushun, Joshua was there waiting. When he received his teacher's paycheck, he took her out to eat. When his money ran out, he cooked for her in his family's small apartment. The first time she saw it she tried to mask her surprise. In the stark room where he lived with his family there was a table, a storage cabinet, and a bed that had replaced the old *kang*. Joshua's family was now the only one in the neighborhood that had heat, thanks to his father's status at the factory. A technician, Zhong Wei

Quan was often called out in the middle of the night to fix broken machinery, and installing heat was the factory's way of compensating him. But the Zhong family had no refrigerator or toilet. The family shared a public restroom with their neighbors.

Some evenings Joshua would show up at Li Li's apartment in time to carry the groceries upstairs for her mother. He was unlike any Chinese man Li Li had ever known. He would shoo her mother out of the kitchen and go to work expertly chopping vegetables that he stir-fried in a wok. They ate together at the dining table, but it seemed Joshua was forever popping up, offering to get her something. After the meal was cleared away, he insisted on washing and drying the dishes. On weekends, he came by to help Li Li's mother wash clothes and clean the house. He would do anything for a chance to see his beloved.

At breakfast one morning before Li Li left town on business, her mother pressed her about Joshua. Li Li glanced up, but kept eating.

"You need someone like him," Liang Zhen told her daughter, her voice persistent.

"What do you mean by that?"

"I spoiled you," her mother said. "You need someone who can take care of you."

"I can take care of myself," Li Li declared.

Exasperated, her mother threw up her arms. "Where else will you find a man who will cook and clean for you?" she asked.

"Mama," she groaned, grabbing her suit jacket and dashing out the door.

Joshua lifted his head from the book on his desk and blinked to adjust to the dimness of the closet-sized study space his father had built for him in their apartment. His eyes stopped on the black-and-white school picture of Li Li. His heart heavy, he put on his glasses and peered into the face of the young woman with long hair cascading onto her shoulders. Her image stared pensively back at him. He turned over the picture to read her words again. Neatly inscribed in Chinese characters were the calm, sure lines of a poem she had written him:

Cai yu ren jiao bian ren xin,
gao shan liu shui xiang gu jin.

To build an everlasting relationship like the fresh river
and the mountain that follow each other forever,
we must have time to examine each other's hearts.

Reading her words was agonizing. More than anything else, he wanted this woman to be his wife, but for now he couldn't have her.

How long?

At the sound of a soft footstep, he glanced up from the picture. It was his little sister, Xia. From the sadness in his eyes, she knew where his mind and heart had been.

"Why do you keep chasing after that girl?" she asked. She couldn't understand it when there were so many other girls to choose from. Her brother was well-known in the community as a graduate of Dalian Foreign Language Institute, a top student in high school, the commander of Youth Pioneers and the chair of the Youth League.

"I have to," he said, refusing to admit defeat. "You wouldn't understand."

"You have to stop," she begged. "When will you figure it out?"

"Figure what out?"

"It's obvious," she said, a note of anger rising in her voice. "Everyone knows but you. You are wasting your time. Her family will never accept you."

Sheng er da xi.
Sheng nu xiao xi.

It is a great happiness to have a son.
It is a small happiness to have a daughter.

TWO

BORN OF REVOLUTION

Outside the train window, Li Li watched the green rice paddies roll by. Somewhere across the countryside, another client of the Fushun Law Firm II was awaiting her arrival to negotiate a contract for his company.

Into her mind came an image of the grandfather in whose footsteps she had followed. She imagined him sitting in the seat of judgment as a Supreme Court justice in the Guangxi Province where her mother grew up. What went through this respected lawyer's mind, she wondered, when the daughter he had sent to a private Catholic high school ran away at sixteen to become a singer and a dancer in Mao's army?

Lost in thought, Li Li gazed out at a slow-moving river that wound through the countryside. What powerful pull had given her mother the strength to give up the fame of her family and security of her home to join a cause that would change the world? What iron will had driven her to demand an abortion when she felt she couldn't bring another life into the upheaval of her world?

Li Li pondered how the story of her mother's life was now woven into hers. There was a sense that from some unknown place, something Li Li could not begin to understand was pulling her along.

At thirty, Liu Liang Zhen was already the mother of one child, and she did not want another. In a time of great famine, another child meant another life to feed, nurture, and worry about.

Li Li's mother had grown up an independent woman. She defied her stepmother's wishes that she attend medical school to become a healer like her father, a judge widely known for his herbal-medicine gifts. Instead, swept up in the revolutionary fervor that was gripping China, Liang Zhen ran off with her girlfriends to join the People's Liberation Army.

Her job was to sing and dance for the soldiers before they marched off to fight the Nationalist Kuomintang, inspiring them to bravery on the battlefield. A war song written by one of her army friends was her favorite:

Wo shi yi ge bing lai zi liao bai xing.
Da bai le ri ben qin lue zhe!
Xiao mie le jiang fei jun!

I am a soldier of the common people.
Take the Japanese out of our land!
Chase Chiang Kai-shek to Taiwan!

When the triumphant, surviving soldiers returned from battle, Liang Zhen and the dancers showered them with flowers. They pinned tags to their comrades' uniforms, declaring them war heroes. For months, she sang the soldiers back onto the battlefield until in 1949 the communist army forced Chiang Kai-shek and his Kuomintang from the mainland to Taiwan, bringing the devastating civil war to an end.

Three hundred thousand people gathered in Beijing's Tiananmen Square on October 1, 1949, to witness Mao proclaim the founding of the People's Republic of China. Like the turmoil that would follow under Mao's rule, Liang Zhen's life was far from settled. The following year, she was transferred to the Qi Dong army base in the central province of Hunan. She arrived with her hair neatly tied in long black braids and her Russian army uniform cinched with a belt at the waist. Li Li's father, Nie Guang Qian, was one of the first soldiers she met.

Guang Qian was born in 1930 in Shanghai, the city where Li Li's grandfather, Nie De Sheng, sought his fortune and lost it. De Sheng was the editor of the *Commercial Monthly* business newspaper when his hunger to be an entrepreneur grew insatiable. He staked all he had to buy a ship to transport commercial products from Shanghai to Wuhan, a city five hundred miles west up the Yangtze River.

It was a disaster. His lack of business acumen and his naiveté about the rules of trade cost him his entire cargo. After his ship arrived, but before he could sell the goods in his first shipment to Wuhan, the locals robbed him of everything. His creditors took him to court, and De Sheng was ordered to pay 40 percent of the loss. The penalty would have been even stiffer were it not for his well-connected brother, Nie Yong Tai. Li Li's grand-uncle was not only the owner of the biggest silk factory in Shanghai, he was married to the daughter of Zeng Guo Fan, a famous Chinese military hero admired for his ability to preserve order during the ruthless Qing Dynasty in the late nineteenth century.

Bankrupt, Li Li's grandfather had nowhere to go but to a village that bore the name of his ancestors near Hengshan in Hunan Province. Unable to afford passage on a commercial boat, he boarded Guang Qian and the rest of the family on a slow boat from Shanghai up the 3,900-mile Yangtze. For a month they floated on China's longest river before arriving in Hengshan, where for generations the Nie family had leased their land to local rice farmers. Little did Guang Qian's father know of the eventual repercussions of his decision to return to the village where his family had been landlords.

Guang Qian's ancestors were famous in the village of Nie. At the village entrance stood several *pai lou,* stone memorial gates erected by edict of the emperor to honor Nie ancestors who had demonstrated the highest knowledge and virtues in the kingdom. The grantee's level of accomplishment strictly dictated the height, width, and elaborateness of decoration of each *pai lou.* Hand-carved in the stone arches were the names of Nies who had served as Cabinet ministers as far back as the Song Dynasty in the thirteenth century, along with words from the emperor recognizing the Nies' purity, benevolence, and contributions to the dynasty.

The Nie landlords provided De Sheng's family with housing in the village, where he taught literature and calligraphy. Within a few years, he was able to pass the rigorous government examination in Nanjing to become a government official. He was assigned to a post in Chongqing, six hundred miles to the northwest of the village of Nie. Li Li's grandmother, Nie Li Song Shou, whose ability to read and write was rare for Chinese women in the 1930s, raised their five sons and two daughters while he was away.

Born in the waning days of the Qing Dynasty, Song Shou was among the last of China's daughters subjected to the thousand-year-old tradition of foot binding. As a young child, Song Shou winced in pain as long strips of cloth bound her turned-under toes to the bottom of each foot, leaving only her big toe extended for balance. For three years, she endured the excruciating binding. Slowly, it broke her arches, causing her deformed feet to shrink. The three-inch feet, reverently referred to as golden lilies, were considered the height of beauty. Tiny feet made a young Chinese woman most desirable for marriage.

They also severely impaired Song Shou's ability to walk. For the rest of her life, Song Shou hobbled along slowly on the outside edges of her feet. So difficult was it for her to walk that her husband hired a litter and four men to carry her several miles to Hengshan to buy food for the family.

She was not home that day in 1938 when Guang Qian and his older brother and younger sister heard the warning cries from frantic villagers.

"Hide! The Japanese are here!"

Li Li's father was eight, and it was the height of the Sino-Japanese War. The invaders were cutting a swath of violence through China, terrorizing and murdering civilians as they went.

Terrified, Guang Qian clambered up on the family's roof to hide where he could watch. Below him, he saw a small figure dash into the open. It was his frightened six-year-old sister fleeing from their house. Within seconds, he saw a Japanese soldier take aim. Almost simultaneously he heard the crack of the rifle and saw his sister crumple to the ground. In a panic, Guang Qian waited for the soldier to turn away, then he leaped off the roof, knocking off a loose stone shingle, which crashed down on his face and slashed his cheekbone. He scrambled to his sister, choking back his fear. In an instant he could see she was badly wounded. Knowing the soldiers still were nearby, he dragged her back to the coverage of their home. Trembling, he turned her over and found that a bullet had ripped through her ribcage. He grasped desperately at her side, trying to stop the steady flow of blood, but he knew he was powerless to save her. She died cradled in his arms.

When his horrified mother returned, she gathered her remaining children and fled into the mountains, where they hid until the Japanese were gone.

Barely three years later, Song Shou was mourning the devastating loss of another loved one. Her husband died of cancer when Guang Qian was eleven, leaving her with barely enough money to feed her family. The rides in the litter came to an end. Song Shou hobbled seven miles to and from Hengshan each week to sell her homegrown vegetables in order to buy food and medicine for her children. At night, she soaked her throbbing feet in hot water to relieve the pain. Still, not once did Guang Qian hear his mother complain.

In 1948, the year he graduated from high school, Li Li's father carefully cut one of his mother's blankets in half to make a bedroll. Then he slipped out the back door unnoticed. It was only when she received his first letter weeks later that his worried mother learned what had become of her eighteen-year-old son. He was now a soldier in the People's Liberation Army.

The young man was eager to join the revolutionary cause. Soldiers who could read and write Mao's messages were in demand. Like thousands of other young people, Guang Qian put his hope in the forceful leader, believing that the communists could rebuild a nation torn apart by corruption, foreign invasion, and civil war.

By 1949, most of the Kuomintang had fled to Taiwan, but some remained in hiding, often carrying out guerrilla-style attacks. Guang Qian was assigned to sweep across the mountains of western Hunan, clearing out those enemy soldiers who remained. At twenty, he earned a medal for his bravery.

It was when he returned from his mountain patrol to his base in Qi Dong that he first saw the young soldier who would become his wife. She arrived with another teenage girl, but Guang Qian's attention was drawn solely to Liang Zhen. Her wide smile and the fine skin of her oval face were imprinted on his heart, an image he could still conjure decades later. Although Guang Qian was tall and handsome in his army uniform, Liang Zhen would later have no memory whatsoever of that first meeting. But Guang Qian was not easily deterred.

Liang Zhen was accustomed to being noticed. A talented beauty in high school in Guilin, a southern city also known for its natural beauty, she was a gifted musician. She also was smart. Her decision to join Mao's army instead of going to college was one she would later regret. While she wrestled with the horrors of war, her younger brothers became doctors. Not only did her choice disappoint her stepmother, but she broke her father's heart.

Li Li's grandfather, Liu Zhi Hua, reached the pinnacle of legal power in Guangxi Province when he was named to head the Supreme Court. He had graduated from the prestigious Peking University and studied law in Tokyo. As head of the province's highest court, he oversaw landmark decisions that charted the law in the time of Old China. But it was the Chinese herbal medicine he practiced from his home that earned the highest respect in his community. When an illness became an emergency, neighbors came late into the night to the Liu home asking for Zhi Hua to prescribe an herbal cure.

Liang Zhen's father had good reason to worry when his daughter joined the army. After Mao came to power, her life in the army became far harsher. The unit she and Guang Qian served in was ordered to move north to Liaoning Province in northeastern China. There she was recruited for China's Volunteer Army to serve on a deadlier battlefront. Before Liang Zhen boarded the train to the war zone in North Korea, Guang Qian proposed to the beautiful young soldier. Her acceptance was the thread that for five years linked them across miles and hardship.

Guang Qian, who had become one of the army's youngest colonels, was bitterly disappointed when the army refused to let him go the war front. Now that the communists were in charge, his father's status as the son of a landlord would become an inescapable curse. At best, it marked him untrustworthy;

at worst, he was considered a traitor. Never in his military career would he be allowed to fight the enemy on the front lines.

The hardships Li Li's mother faced in North Korea at times seemed unbearable. In a small village where the Chinese soldiers were fed, she spent the freezing winter hauling water from a river in heavy buckets hung from a bamboo pole slung across her shoulders. Like the other communist soldiers, she wore a cotton uniform, which was nearly impossible to dry in the cold once it was wet. On their feet they wore canvas shoes, and few had gloves. When they were lucky, they found shelter in the homes of the villagers, who taught them how to speak Korean. Sometimes they slept in a rock cave or outside in minus twenty degrees Fahrenheit weather, unable to build fires for fear of attracting the attention of the enemy. Many suffered frostbite on their feet, hands, and faces. Food was scarce, and hot food was rare. They ate *shaobing,* a hard, unleavened bread, millet, and beans. Liang Zhen was one of many who suffered digestive diseases that would plague them for the rest of their lives. But amid the hardship, Liang Zhen also forged friendships that would last a lifetime. Luo Rui Fen and Liang Zhen danced and sang side by side for the Chinese soldiers, becoming best friends — friends that would help one another decades later.

Liang Zhen's black braids grew down to her waist. At night she changed into the long full skirts the Korean girls wore to dance for the soldiers. They performed in a nearby cave used as a hideout to conceal the communists from the Americans. One evening, several dozen soldiers squeezed into the small rock enclosure. They blocked the narrow entryway, crushing the dancers against the back wall. Unable to breathe, the women panicked and several fainted. Liang Zhen feared she would die. Suddenly a rifle shot rang out, silencing the rowdy soldiers. A commander bellowed, "Back off!" An airway opened, and the terrified dancers could breathe again. During the long days and nights in North Korea, Liang Zhen had sometimes feared dying of cold or hunger, but never had she imagined suffocating to death in a cave.

A few years into the conflict, Guang Qian was crushed to see a report that a young woman identified by only her surname, Liu, had been killed near the front lines. He tried desperately to find more details, but to no avail. The news left him shaking with grief — he was certain his love was gone forever.

In 1955, the communists and the Americans accepted a cease-fire, ending the bloodshed that had bathed Northern Korea. By then, an estimated 2.8 million soldiers and civilians were dead. Thousands of Chinese soldiers who survived the terrible war were sick from digestive diseases. They returned to their homeland on foot, in trucks, and on trains. The government gave them a hero's welcome, proclaiming victory for the communist cause.

Amid the waves of returning forces, Guang Qian always kept a hopeful eye. Finally, one day near the North Korean border his hope erupted into joy. There amid the sea of soldiers was a thin, exhausted Liang Zhen. Through his tears, Guang Qian pressed through the crowd and embraced his love. They were just two of the millions who had been separated from loved ones, and it seemed a miracle she was still alive.

The years of waiting were over. They were married in Haicheng, and the next spring in Shengyang their first daughter was born. Looking back at all they had survived, they finally felt some sense of relief.

But soon it was Guang Qian whose life was threatened. He developed a severe respiratory illness that the army doctors, who practiced only Western medicine, pronounced incurable. Desperate, Liang Zhen appealed to her father for help. She took his prescription to a Chinese medicine store, then boiled the herbal mixture she was given in a pot of soup. Guang Qian took the remedy, and within days his father-in-law's herbal potion healed him.

It was seven years later when Liang Zhen, working round the clock in Yingkou, learned she was pregnant again.

Her daughter Ke Ke returned home from the child-care center at the end of each week homesick and hungry. One Saturday, Liang Zhen made her rice soup. But when Ke Ke saw the rice floating in the watery soup with no vegetables, she cried in despair. She'd had nothing but a rice porridge called *congee* to eat that week for breakfast, lunch, and dinner. In the countryside, things were even worse for the starving peasants who could find no food at all. They were stripping leaves from trees and eating them to stay alive. The communist dictator's relentless drive to industrialize China overnight was exacting a horrific price.

Yet Mao had no sympathy for the people he was starving.

"Having only tree leaves to eat? So be it," he was quoted as saying.

The average Chinese adult at the time was eating about fifteen hundred calories daily, about half the intake of a typical American. Liang Zhen knew she was fortunate to be fed food provided in the cafeteria to workers who often slept at their workplace so they could labor day and night for Mao. But she had her own fears about survival.

She had suffered several miscarriages since the birth of her first daughter, and her own mother had died in childbirth, leaving her motherless just moments after she was born. Her nagging stomach problems since her days in North Korea refused to go away, and she was determined not to do anything that would risk her health or threaten her job. Alone one day, she boarded the train to the army hospital. With her she carried a letter obtained by her husband from army headquarters recommending that she be allowed to have an abortion.

Abortion and abandonment had been common throughout China's long history of political upheaval. Even Mao and his second wife were said to have abandoned their own baby in the 1930s during the Red Army's Long March.

Abandonment was something that would never cross Liang Zhen's mind. And the possibility of having a son, a traditional Chinese family's greatest hope, was no incentive for her to have this baby. It did not matter to her whether the child was a boy or girl. Long ago, she'd rejected the ancient proverb she'd heard so often:

Sheng er da xi.
Sheng nu xiao xi.

It is a great happiness to have a son.
It is a small happiness to have a daughter.

In the Year of the Rabbit, Liang Zhen gave birth to another girl. To her mother, Li Li was an ugly baby. She was dark and hairy — not at all like her sister, a beautiful baby that the hospital nurses had fought to hold. Worse yet, she was often fussy, crying out many times during the night. Exhausted from working, Liang Zhen would wake up her eldest daughter and ask her to rock the crib until the baby Li Li finally fell back to sleep.

~

Li Li had just started walking the year her father was reassigned to the People's Liberation Army station in Fushun, a few hundred miles to the northeast. When Guang Qian left his family behind in Yingkou, Liang Zhen's stepmother traveled alone more than one thousand miles by slow-moving train from her home in Guilin in Guangxi Province to care for her young granddaughter. Li Li would never get the chance to meet her grandfather the lawyer, who had died the year she was born.

Grandma Qin prepared delicious hot meals, unlike her stepdaughter who joined the army before she learned to cook. Li Li's favorite was chicken soup with *xian gu,* Guilin's famous black mushrooms. As the sweet mushrooms and the poultry simmered in the steaming broth, she watched her grandmother drop in dried dragon eye, chestnuts, orange peels, and dried rice noodles. Last came the *fu ru,* the salty tofu made in the Guilin factory where her grandmother once worked, and the mysterious mixture of Chinese medicine herbs concocted by her grandfather.

For two years while her mother worked, Li Li was raised by the grandmother she called *Lao Lao.* She told stories to Li Li, sang her lullabies, and potty-trained her. In the Chinese tradition, Li Li wore split leggings so she could be easily swept up and held over the toilet hole in the floor. When she played, the toddler wore a special half-skirt hand-sewn by Grandma Qin, who wanted to make sure her granddaughter would not hit her bare bottom when she fell to the dirt floor. When it came time for Grandma Qin to return to Guilin, Li Li refused to believe she was gone. She opened closets and drawers and searched under the bed and table, calling out for *Lao Lao.*

Without Grandma Qin to help, Li Li's parents sought the services of a nanny. The woman they interviewed had grown up in the cold northeast, where she slept only on a *kang.* She steadfastly refused to become the family's live-in nanny unless she was provided a *kang* to sleep on. Guang Qian, who grew up in the warmth of southern China, had never seen such a thing.

Regardless, he did what he must. He talked with neighbors and found an old farmer who could help. He then built a *kang,* and the nanny approved.

The nanny settled into their home, the only single-family house Li Li would ever occupy in China. Unlike the apartments Li Li's family would later live in, the house in Yingkou on Bohai Bay, an arm of the Yellow Sea, had both a front and a back yard. In the wake of the Great Famine, Guang Qian believed that any piece of land not planted in fruits and vegetables was wasted. He planted grape vines in the front yard, which also was home to the family's chickens that often fought Li Li for her father's grapes. She would drag out a wooden stool so that she could reach her prize. But as she stretched up to pick a grape, a chicken would leap into the air, flapping its wings wildly, and snatch the fruit from her tiny hand, sometimes with such force she was knocked down to the ground. But Li Li was happy to meet the feisty chickens' challenge. Popping the grapes into her mouth before they could steal them soon became a favorite game.

What was most alluring, though, was the forbidden bridge in front of her house. That bridge crossed the silent flow of a river and led to the world beyond the secure life of her family.

The first time she sneaked out of the yard she was three. Clutching her doll, she walked across the wide bridge into a strange, unexplored realm, leaving behind her quiet neighborhood. Soon her nanny was desperately searching for her, increasingly frantic when she couldn't find her. But those emotions paled next to Liang Zhen's anger when she returned home to find her youngest daughter still missing.

Eventually Li Li reappeared from her wandering, crossing back over the bridge empty-handed.

Her relieved mother scolded her. "Why did you leave the yard? Where is your doll?"

Li Li told her someone took it, blaming the rag-pickers who wandered the streets scavenging paper and other scraps of trash to reuse.

But later, Li Li could not wipe the memory of her doll from her mind. Losing it nagged at her, and in her mind she could hear the words her father taught her: "Never throw anything away."

Her father had learned in the army to take good care of everything he had.

"You have it today, but you may not have it tomorrow," he warned her. "It is not easy to have it, so always appreciate it."

The doll haunted her. One day, when no one was watching, Li Li ventured across the bridge once again to try to find the lost doll. The impossible odds of bringing her baby doll home and her mother's warnings about the dangers of the world beyond the bridge did not stop her. She had a mission, and she had no fear of the unknown.

In 1966, Li Li's family joined her father in Fushun, the industrial city that had become instrumental to Mao's march toward modernization. It was the beginning of the Great Proletariat Cultural Revolution born out of the communist dictator's maniacal need to regain control of the Communist Party. Mao was in a power struggle with his rivals in the wake of his disastrous attempts to push China into world domination regardless of the consequences. Believing that revolution was a necessity for China's move forward, he kept his country in a perpetual state of turmoil. He ordered a massive youth mobilization led by the Red Guard to wage class war against "traditional society" and the "old systems" he accused his rivals of representing. In order to march into the future, they attacked the "Four Olds" of society: old ideas, old cultures, old manners, and old customs. The roaming brigades of militant students who wore red armbands patrolled the neighborhoods, humiliating and shaming landlords and others branded as capitalists. The Red Guard struck fear in the hearts of local residents as their activities became increasingly violent.

It was during the birth of the Red Guard that the Nie family moved into a one-room apartment in an army office building where Guang Qian worked. They shared a public toilet with the other army personnel and they had no kitchen, but the army cafeteria provided plenty to eat at a time when much of Fushun's population was desperate for food. The building they shared with the police was secure, and safety was something very few in Fushun could count on.

Across the Hun River, living in a one-room apartment without heat, Joshua was not so fortunate. He was born in 1962 on January 13, a date he considered so unlucky that he later changed it to the twelfth. At the time, it was the custom of Chinese mothers to eat one hundred eggs in the thirty days following childbirth to regain all the strength they had lost. In the month after Joshua was born, his mother ate all that their family had — just eighteen eggs. When she stopped nursing him at three months, there was no money to buy milk.

In the wake of the Great Famine, China was still suffering a severe food shortage. The communist government responded by restricting the amount of food its people could have. A strict rationing program was enforced, and Joshua lived much of his childhood worrying about food. Children under eighteen were allotted twenty-seven and a half pounds of food per month, less than a pound each day. Adults without work were allowed thirty pounds; working adults received thirty-three. Most of the food allotment was *chu liang,* the rough corn that Joshua's mother used to make the cornbread that her children ate for breakfast, lunch, and dinner. Joshua hated it. Ten percent of the allotment was *xi liang,* the fine wheat that his mother hoarded away until she'd saved enough to make dumplings for Chinese New Year.

There was no fruit available in the market in the winter, and even in the summer, when Joshua occasionally spotted watermelon, apples, or pears, his family could not afford them. The only vegetables they had to eat were the dried turnips and the leaves of cabbage that Joshua and his brothers managed to scavenge.

When they heard the clip-clop of horses and the rumble of wooden wagon wheels on their street, the boys dropped what they were doing and dashed out of their home. The huge wagon was piled eight feet high with cabbages from the countryside. The brothers joined the sons of neighbors who ran alongside the wagon picking off the leaves. The angry driver cursed at them, but the running boys kept peeling away the leaves until the driver pulled the four-horse team to a halt and leaped down to the street to chase after them.

Joshua's mother did not reprimand them. She chopped up the scavenged cabbage leaves and measured out just enough of the rationed flour she'd squirreled away to make dumplings for the family. Still, it was not enough to satisfy them.

There was no money for store-bought clothes for the children, and cloth, like food, was rationed. Each month, Joshua's mother set aside the yards of cloth allotted for her four children. Then, for Chinese New Year, she pulled out the cloth and relied on a skill she learned long ago. At the age of sixteen, her stepmother had told her it was time to leave home. She found work in a factory, where she learned to sew. At the start of each new year, Joshua's mother would sew one new set of clothes for each of her sons and her daughter.

Joshua's mother had no memory of her birth name. She was six and her sister was eleven when they were taken from their biological parents' home. All that she could remember was that a man she did not know burst into their house early one morning after her father left for his job as a carpenter. The man spoke harshly to their mother, and the frightened girls didn't understand what was happening. He took their mother and the girls from their home in Kaifeng in central Henan Province by train about five hundred miles north and east to Tianjin near Beijing. When they reached the house of a couple who were strangers, their mother left them. The abandoned sisters huddled together and cried. A few days later, their mother returned. She held her terrified daughters close to her and told them goodbye. The strangers adopted them and gave them new names — Wang Kun for Joshua's mother, and Xiao Liu for her sister — but treated them like servants. The sisters never saw their mother or father again.

Thrown into the foreign home, the girls clung to one another for comfort until the following year when Wang Kun lost the last tie to her family. Her sister Xiao Liu died of tuberculosis at age twelve. Wang Kun was left alone with stepparents she barely knew. They did not allow her to go to school, and her days were weighed down by loneliness as she carried out her household chores.

Soon she would have no more time to ponder her misery and desire to be with other children. Her stepparents adopted a one-year-old girl, and Wang

Kun became a nanny at ten. Her stepmother had been told that a couple too poor to feed all seven of their children were giving away their youngest daughter. She offered to pay for the child, but the girl's parents asked only for a bag of flour in exchange for their daughter.

Wang Kun took care of the girl for six years until the day her stepmother announced it was time for her to get a job. She took Wang Kun to Fushun, where she had heard there was work for unskilled girls in a cloth factory. She dropped her stepdaughter at the factory dormitory, and once again Wang Kun was left on her own.

It was in the factory where she learned to be a seamstress that she found a husband. She met Zhong Wei Quan one day when her sewing machine broke down. He was the technician who came to fix it, and she later learned that the handsome young man was the son of a farmer from the countryside of Xiao Dong Zhou. Like thousands of other peasants, he had quit school after eighth grade and soon set off to the city in search of work. She was twenty and he was twenty-eight when the two married in 1954.

Even as a wife and mother under the protection of her husband, Wang Kun's terrible childhood fear of intruders never left her. When night came to Fushun during the chaotic Cultural Revolution, that fear took over. She bolted the doors on the windows and locked the doors of their house. She slept in terror that street marauders firing guns and cannons stolen from the military arsenal would break in and kill one of her children. If someone knocked on the door, she told her husband not to answer. Even during the day she was afraid for her children, and often rightfully so. One afternoon, when Joshua was five, he and his brother were walking home alone and gunfire shattered the quiet in the street. The boys ran for cover, hiding behind the corner of a wall. Joshua peered out to see what was happening. A bullet zinged by just above his head. The brash street fighters were on the prowl again in the poor neighborhood, and no one was safe.

Mao encouraged the fighting by rallying his allies to take on those he deemed leftists. The dictator's reckless rule over China was based on creating a revolutionary fervor, and during the Cultural Revolution he created chaos and upheaval by carving the Chinese population into groups according to their social status and political beliefs. Joshua's parents were Red, Mao's designation for common laborers, peasants, and soldiers who were praised as the foundation of the communist society. Li Li's father served in the military, but his landlord background made his family Black, the enemy of communism. Black families fell into five categories, and landlords were enemy number one, worse than criminals, counter-revolutionaries, rightists, and capitalists.

Although his own parents were landlords, Mao hated landlords. He created the Red Guards to terrorize them and others viewed as capitalists. Their homes often were ransacked and possessions confiscated. The once-revered elders were brought down by the young militants. One day when he was in elementary school, Joshua watched Red Guards in their early twenties drag a once-respected company official up a six-foot bamboo scaffold. Hands tied behind his back, the official wore a dunce cap and a sign that read, "Follower of Capitalism. Enemy of the Proletariat." The humiliated man knelt down on the wooden board, and for eight long hours the Red Guards taunted him, screaming names in his ear, spitting in his face, and laughing at him. Joshua was mortified.

Accused of being sons of a landlord, Li Li's father and his brothers were targets of another common form of intimidation. Behind closed doors, officials interrogated them repeatedly. Guang Qian's younger brother was accused of criticizing the People's Liberation Army. His older brother, an engineer, was jailed for criticizing Russia's communist engineers. In those years, truth was irrelevant. All it took was an accusation or the mere appearance of disloyalty to Mao or his hard-line communism for the Red Guard to come down hard and quick. Even criticism of Mao's Russian allies was considered rightist and warranted harassment from his ruthless squads.

Guang Qian's older brother had changed his name to Gang Feng to hide his landlord background so that he could serve in the Korean War. But his faithful army service was ignored when he refused to admit that it was wrong to criticize a Russian engineer's design work. He was ordered to a labor camp in a suburb of Nanjing, the site of the Japanese slaughter that had killed two hundred and fifty thousand Chinese three decades before.

Once a month, depending on the changing political situation, he was permitted to board the bus to Nanjing on a Sunday to visit his wife and children. Over and over again, the communists told Gang Feng they would release him if he would apologize for his criticism of the Russians. He lost twenty-three years of his life in the work camp, stoically insisting he had done no wrong.

~

Guang Qian's sessions before the army interrogation committee in Fushun felt like facing a firing squad. Without warning, he would be dragged before the committee to be questioned once again about being the son of a landlord: "Where did you grow up? What education did you receive from your father? What relationship do you have with your brothers?"

Often, the interrogations would last late into the night. By the time he returned home, Li Li and her sister had gone to bed. But they could hear the fear in their father's voice as he and their mother talked in hushed murmurs.

The parents were not only worried about the interrogations, they feared for their daughters' safety. Until now, the presence of the military and security police in their building had offered protection from the violence in the streets of Fushun. But the revolutionaries who opposed the army had threatened to burn down the residences of army soldiers. Li Li's parents felt like they had no choice. The only way to keep their daughters out of danger was to send them away to live in the countryside.

For nearly a year, the sisters lived an hour's train ride from the city in the home of the family of her mother's friend. The kind old woman told Li Li and Ke Ke to call her Grandma Liu. Her youngest daughter took care of Li Li, braiding her hair, telling her stories, and teaching her children's songs. To the sisters from the city, the countryside was full of novelties. Each morning, they watched Grandma Liu milk the goats and chase the chickens around the backyard until she caught one and killed it for dinner. While the bird cooked on the stove, they watched her chop vegetables and make her delicious dumplings. At night, Li Li slept on the *kang* with her sister, Grandma Liu, and the family. It was the only time in her life she would sleep in a bed with six people.

On weekends, Liang Zhen came to visit, always returning to the city without her daughters. Li Li wondered why she didn't stay, but her mother would not explain. Some days, both her parents came, and the excited sisters would share the latest happenings at Grandma Liu's. Their parents said little about Fushun. The girls had no idea what was happening there until the day their parents arrived to take them home.

Li Li watched wistfully as Grandma Liu waved goodbye in front of the house where the sisters had lived peacefully for so many months. At the same time, she was relieved that her family would be together again at home. But what she saw when she arrived in Fushun shocked her. Bullets were lodged in the walls of their building and the glass in the hallway windows was blasted out. Her parents explained that the building had been shut down and sealed off after some trouble in the streets. Soon they packed up their belongings and left the filthy building, moving to an apartment north of the Hun River, several miles from the neighborhood where Joshua's family lived.

Li Li didn't know it, but at work her father remained under siege. Her parents were so distracted by the interrogations and the demands of their jobs that they neglected the most basic of tasks. Li Li was seven when she mentioned that her friends were no longer at the child-care center. It was only then that her parents realized they had forgotten to enroll her in kindergarten.

On her first day of school, she took a test in *pinyin,* the system for using the Western alphabet to spell out Chinese words. That day she brought home a D. She was embarrassed, and her father was upset. By then, he had taught her hundreds of the three thousand Chinese characters that students must know to graduate from high school. But she had not ever seen Chinese words written in the English alphabet. He gave Li Li her first lesson in *pinyin* at home that night. They sat together on the bed, and he patiently wrote the Chinese characters followed by the *pinyin* words for "Long Life to Chairman Mao" — *Mao Zhu Xi Wan Sui.* He was a strict teacher, and she had a good memory. She quickly mastered *pinyin* and leapt to the head of her class, where she remained the rest of her school career.

It was in elementary school that Li Li began her formal education in communism and the Cultural Revolution's campaign to destroy the "Four Olds." Over the blackboard in each classroom hung a portrait of Chairman Mao. On the chalkboard was his slogan:

Hao hao xue xi tian tian xiang shang.
Study hard and improve every day.

Textbooks began with a page of Mao's famous sayings. In some classrooms, instead of textbooks the students read mimeographed handouts of Mao's messages. They studied from the *Precious Red Book, Selected Quotations from the Writings of Mao.* Li Li and her fellow students toted school-issued wooden guns as they marched into the building. Some days, they watched propaganda films aggrandizing the Cultural Revolution.

Li Li belonged to the Little Red Guards, grade-school students who carried Mao's Little Red Book with them everywhere to memorize the chairman's words. Their role model was Lei Feng, the man touted as Mao's model soldier. He cleaned floors and performed other manual labor without complaint in service to the dictator known as the Great Helmsman. The Little Red Guards were encouraged to do their part to serve the cause of communism by helping older and disabled people in their neighborhoods. In their apartment building, Li Li and her friends escorted the elderly up the stairs to their homes, helped with meals, and swept the community public areas.

But in Joshua's neighborhood, young people became tools for intimidation. The Cultural Revolution gave them permission to be bullies. Students were urged by the communists to criticize teachers who were blamed for teaching capitalism instead of socialism. There were no lessons at all on days that the fearful teachers stayed home. School windows were broken, and the unsupervised students fought among themselves. On the streets, Joshua and his classmates carried wooden spears and wore the red ties of the Youth Pioneers, giving them authority to stop other students and pedestrians. The Pioneers refused to let those they harassed go until their victims memorized and recited quotations from the Little Red Book.

A more serious witch hunt was underway in the factory where Joshua's father was a technician supervising twenty workers. Encouraged to revolt and criticize their leaders, the workers accused Zhong Wei Quan of sabotaging the machinery instead of fixing it.

The relentless persecution continued until one day when Joshua's father broke down. He came home from work, closed the windows, and cried. Joshua laid his head in his father's lap and wept with him. Wei Quan returned to work determined to endure the cruel intimidation no matter how hard it got, and ultimately, he outlasted his tormentors.

The army interrogation committee's questioning of Li Li's father intensified, and sometimes he was detained overnight. Over and over, Guang Qian's interrogators would order him to recall the details of his childhood and his relationship with his two brothers who had been labeled rightists.

One day in 1971, he was slapped with the news he was dreading. The military ordered that Guang Qian be stripped of his colonel status and kicked out of the army. Humiliated, he refused the order, protesting that it was unjustified. For nearly a year he fought to keep his position, stubbornly refusing to accept the government job he was offered. Instead, he stayed home, building wooden tables and chairs while his wife worked and his daughters went to school. Many evenings, to pass the time, he read to Li Li from the few books that he had managed to salvage. Those that were banned, including the teachings of Confucius, he kept by the stove, ready to burn them in an instant if anyone connected to the army or the government came to visit.

During those painful days, Guang Qian often thought of giving in and taking the government job, but he knew that the persecution would never end. His landlord background had become too complicated. One day when Li Li arrived home, he told her they were going to take a trip to visit Grandma Qin. In reality, the purpose of the journey to Guilin was to investigate the possibility of starting a new life in the city where his wife had grown up.

For four days and three nights, Li Li and her father traveled southwest by train until they finally reached the home of the grandmother she so longed to see. While her father went into the city, Li Li sat quietly on the banks of the Li River, listening to the wise old woman as she washed their clothes and the vegetables. She warned her granddaughter about the dangers of fire and water. "Don't touch them," she said. "They can hurt you." Later, when they took a boat from Guilin to Yangshuo to see the famous mountain scenery, Li Li sat by her grandmother's side with her hands folded in her lap as the other children scampered from one side of the boat to the other, dangling their hands in the water. Grandmother Qin looked down at her and smiled. Li Li had learned to listen.

In the afternoons, Grandma Qin would step into the backyard and grab one of her fluttering chickens to kill and cook for dinner. She worked late into the night, bent over her long needle with the heavy thread, stitching together a pair of cloth shoes for her granddaughter. When it came time to board the train for home, Li Li happily wore the soft new shoes *Lao Lao* had embroidered with pink flowers. For her father, though, the long trip back to Fushun was a time of despair. The local government had rejected Guang Qian's request to move his family to Guilin, exercising its right not to accept new residents that it felt its economy could not support.

In 1972, the army processed Guang Qian's dismissal order without his consent. His heart full of bitterness, he began his first government position as a writer for the local mayor. As he expected, the persecution he once suffered in the army continued in his new job, but it took a subtler form. One night from her bedroom, Li Li heard the sounds of her father weeping. The annual review that day from his superiors focused not on the work he had achieved but on his landlord status.

Li Li could hear the sorrow in his voice. "They pointed out my family background again," he told her mother. "They said my brother was a rightist. There's no way I'll get a promotion or a raise."

Liang Zhen listened calmly to her husband's complaints. His landlord background had also affected her career. Once an accountant in a big oil company, she had ended up working in a chemical factory tightening caps onto bottles on the assembly line. Unlike her husband, she was at peace with her life at work, where she had earned the respect of her fellow workers in the factory.

Many times, Guang Qian asked to be transferred to another department, hoping to earn the trust of his new superiors in the government. Repeatedly he would prove that he was a good writer, but his strong mind and sharp tongue always got him into trouble. His new bosses would dredge up his landlord history, and he would move on to another job.

Li Li admired the strong intellect of her father, whose first name meant "humble" and middle name "bright." But she recognized how much pride hurt this man who was in no way humble. He knew the right thing to do was to forgive and move on, but his tongue was ruled by bitterness. As hatred accumulated in his heart, she watched her father's life grow harder, until it seemed he could barely take a step, barely move forward.

In those frustrating years as a government servant, writing at home was her father's consolation. He wrote stories for the People's Liberation Army newspaper, the *Red Flag* magazine, and other communist publications. Late at night and into the morning hours, he sipped his hot tea and wrote novels, plays, and poems.

He was the one who made sure his second daughter learned how to write. With practice and her father's discerning eye, Li Li became good at writing, although she disdained it. To her, it had no value.

"Does it produce anything like the farmer who grows rice and vegetables?" she challenged her father in their debates on the written word. "Does it build anything like the engineer creates new products? Does it save anyone like the doctor who heals his patients?"

"Writing," he patiently tried to persuade his doubtful daughter, "is man's highest calling. Words are the emotional food that feed the hungry heart and the soul."

Li Li was not convinced. She was far more interested in doing something that could save lives and change the world.

Ni zhi dao Ye Su Ji Du ma?

Do you know Jesus Christ?

THREE

THE FORBIDDEN BOOK
1986

J oshua pulled the package from its hiding place and carefully wrapped it in a faded shirt. Slipping it safely into a plain cloth sack, he walked out of his family's apartment. Outside the two-story building, he peered up and down the sidewalk. Seeing no one he knew, he hopped on his bike, relieved that he'd escaped the watchful eyes of neighbors. Darting down the busy streets, he clutched the heavy sack tightly around the handlebars, hoping no one would stop him to talk.

When Li Li answered the door of her apartment, he was breathless, his eyes filled with anticipation. It was time to tell her.

"Are your parents here?" he asked, his voice low.

"No," she said, wondering what was wrong. "Why?"

He looked around one last time as he stepped across the threshold.

"I want to show you something."

"What is it?" she asked.

He pulled the heavy package from the sack, and slowly unwrapped the shirt and unfolded the layers of paper, revealing a thick book. On the cover were two words: Holy Bible.

Li Li had heard of the book that Mao had once banned, but never had she seen one.

"What are you doing with this?" Li Li asked, her eyes flashing.

"I brought it to read to you," he said.

"Why?" she said, bewildered.

"I am a Christian, Li Li," he said quietly.

Her breath caught in her chest. The only religion Mao had ever permitted in communist China was worship of the state. Claiming to be Christian was practically unheard of, let alone sharing the fact with another person.

"How?" she said. "Why?"

The first time he'd ever seen a copy of this forbidden book, he explained, was in 1981 in the library of the foreign language school in the coastal city of Dalian on the southern tip of Liaoning Province.

During a lunch break, he secretly wandered into the area that was restricted to teachers. No librarians were in sight as he slipped down an aisle, scanning the rows of academic titles as he slowly walked along. His eyes locked in on the bottom shelf, and he froze. He peeled his eyes away and furtively looked around. He could not see anyone, and the only thing he could hear was his own breathing. He kneeled down and picked up a book covered in dust.

He knew why this book had for so long gone untouched. Under Mao's rule, simply reading it landed people in prison. But this knowledge was not enough to still his hands. Opening it, a pang of gratefulness washed over him. His years of hard work learning English were now the key that unlocked this elusive treasure. He began to read the words in English. For years he had heard about the book and the value it carried in Western cultures, but to finally hold a Bible in his hands made him shake.

The mysterious book became an irresistible draw to him. Many days, he would sneak into the off-limits area to read it, always at different times to keep from being noticed. A student caught with the Bible could be expelled. But time and again he returned, and time and again he went unnoticed. Months went by before he told anyone about it. It was in a Friendship Store in Dalian that he unexpectedly confided his secret — to an American he had never before met.

The growing seaside city was deluged by foreigners. After years of government restrictions kept them out, they were anxious to visit the country that Deng Xiaoping had opened to the world in 1978, the first time since the communist takeover. When the Americans began pouring in, officials were sent to the foreign-language school to recruit English-speaking tour guides to serve them. Joshua and his classmates were selected to be interns, even though their English was broken and difficult to understand.

He was paid fifteen cents a day to shepherd Americans to historic sites. When the tour bus passed through the poorest part of town, he dutifully told the tourists no one lived in the squalid homes. The foreigners did not know that Joshua and the other guides had been ordered to lie. In fact, the housing was practically unfit for humans. But the locals who lived there had no other choice. Most of China's one billion people made far less than one dollar a day, the world standard for poverty at the time.

Government propaganda claimed that communism had brought a new prosperity to the People's Republic of China. To showcase to the world its economic progress, China built Friendship Stores in major tourist cities. It was in these department stores, where Chinese commoners were not allowed to shop without a permit, that foreigners purchased goods billed as China's best — and often recognized that the stores also offered up a healthy serving of propaganda.

Joshua was waiting at the second floor stairway for a tourist group to finish their souvenir shopping when a Caucasian woman approached him and flashed a small index card.

Ni zhi dao Ye Su Ji Du ma?
Do you know Jesus Christ?

He leaned in toward the well-dressed woman in her sixties. In English, he whispered to her, "I read about him in the Bible, but I want to know more."

The astonished American listened to his story of finding the Bible. Quietly, she talked to the eager young man, marveling at his hunger to learn. Half an hour later, the woman whose name he did not yet know silently prayed, trying not to draw unwanted attention from the plainclothes government officials who patrolled the store. That afternoon Joshua said he wanted to accept Jesus into his life, and he became a Christian.

When the Dalian tour came to an end for the Americans, Joshua went to the harbor to say goodbye. The sampans and tugboats in the Yellow Sea were dwarfed by the mammoth Norwegian Cruise Line ship with its American passengers. The woman who said she was from a state called Florida told him she had something for him. While she rushed back to the ship, Joshua waited with her husband, a huge man who at six foot nine towered over the Chinese. Soon the American woman came hurrying back with a package wrapped in a T-shirt. With her husband's huge figure shielding them from the crowd, she quickly handed Joshua the bundle. He hid it in his jacket.

In his dorm room that night, he closed the door and pulled out the package. Inside the T-shirt was a Bible dictionary in Chinese, along with the woman's name and her address in America.

For the next four years, Joshua corresponded with the wealthy matron in the seaside town of Boca Raton, Florida, who was determined to use her money to save foreign souls.

After his graduation from Dalian in June 1984, he wrote to give her his family's address in Fushun. He was distressed to be returning to the hometown he hated. He could not imagine a lifetime as an English teacher at the local college.

In her letters to him, she was careful not to mention religion. She kept her notes short, hoping not to get the English teacher into trouble. The communist government censors often opened letters and packages postmarked in the United States, and most of the magazines and other English materials she sent him had been opened by the time he received them.

"I told her about you," Joshua said to Li Li after he finished his story.

"What did you say?" she asked, surprised.

"That I was frustrated."

"Why?" she asked, wondering what would make him say such a thing to a stranger.

"I told her it is hard for me to understand the deeper meaning of the Bible," he said. "And it's hard when the woman I want to marry refuses to even consider saying yes."

~

During that summer, Joshua showed Li Li two letters from America. The first was from Boca Raton, Florida, the second came later from Columbia, South Carolina.

When he opened the letter from the Florida woman who had befriended him, his hands were trembling. The words he translated for Li Li at first seemed almost incomprehensible to her. Twice he read the letter aloud before she grasped the magnitude of what it said.

"Come to the United States to study," the letter said. "I will be your sponsor."

"The United States?" Li Li repeated in disbelief. It was the place where Joshua had once heard that people lived in mansions and dollar bills lined the streets.

From that same envelope Joshua pulled out an application for Columbia Bible College in South Carolina.

"Bible college?" Li Li said, confused. Neither of them had ever heard of such a thing.

Before Li Li and Joshua were born, Mao had issued what was called the edict of Religious Reform. The dictator so believed that religion was an opiate for the people that he used his conviction to justify the cruel religious persecution of his people. Thousands of practicing Christians had been arrested and sent to prison. A decade after Chairman Mao's death, people who believed in a God were still dismissed as weak and ignorant.

In her letter, the American woman made her agenda quite clear. If he wished to accept her offer to become his sponsor, she would give him no other choice but to attend the Bible college she supported.

His dream was to attend a university, not Bible college. But Joshua was quick to agree to her terms, unwilling to turn down a chance to study in the land of opportunity. To Li Li, it seemed that Joshua was forever trying to push the boundaries. This appeared to be just another of his wild dreams that would soon be forgotten like the rest of the ideas he hatched.

But later that summer he handed her a second letter, from Columbia Bible College, that contained an offer far beyond anything that even Joshua had imagined.

"Read it to me," she said, handing it back to him.

Over and over he'd reread the words, but still they overwhelmed him.

We are pleased to announce that you have been awarded a scholarship to the graduate school of the Columbia Bible College.

Li Li was awestruck. Joshua had faithfully kept up his correspondence with the American woman he had not seen for four years. Now in this last letter, he received the gift of new life. This shrewd young man who refused to give up was at last about to get what he so badly wanted. He would escape from the grip of his hometown in China to cross over the threshold to America, a place Li Li never in her lifetime expected to see.

"Congratulations!" she said, elated by this good fortune. But inside, she felt the slow sinking weight of the fact that he would be leaving.

"It is time," Joshua spoke up, his voice strong and confident, "for us to be engaged."

She stared into his penetrating eyes. She was face to face with the question of marriage, a prospect that for so long she had kept at a safe distance. Suddenly, it had become a practical issue. Joshua would soon be gone for a year. He could no longer wait.

Li Li's encouraging smile slowed Joshua's hammering heart as she led him into the room where her father sat. Still, Joshua's stomach felt weak and jumpy. Armed with a scholarship to America, he had summoned the courage to approach her father. But he had no idea what would become of his request.

Li Li slipped away to her bedroom, leaving the two alone. The arguments Joshua had rehearsed raced through his mind, but the young man who was never at a loss for words felt his voice falter as he faced her father. Breathing in deeply, he spoke the words he had yearned to say.

"I have come to ask your permission to marry your daughter."

A cloud passed over Guang Qian's face, though not of surprise. He had long expected this day to come. From the start, he did not want his daughter to marry a man beneath her. Throughout China's five-thousand-year history, marriages between mismatched families had been considered taboo, though on rare occasions they occurred. Even after Deng Xiaoping had opened the door to Western influences, it remained of utmost importance to a father weighing a young man's request for marriage that the two families match.

In this case, they definitely did not, and Li Li's father held resolutely to that fact.

Guang Qian's mind was set in stone. He could not imagine anything that could sway him. Then Joshua presented the unimaginable: He had been accepted by a graduate school and would be leaving in two months for America — a place most Chinese people only dreamed of. Guang Qian had never heard of anyone from Fushun, a city of two million, going to this strange land of opportunity that he secretly admired. Against all logic that Li Li's father held dear, he realized that this son of a factory worker had been given a miraculous opportunity. His resistance softened as his eyes opened to the new reality that this young man who once seemed an unthinkable match might someday be worthy of his daughter.

The devotion in Joshua's eyes testified to his determination to make Li Li his wife, no matter the differences in their social status. Guang Qian had seen the flush on Li Li's face that night, but at the time he could only wonder what had finally convinced the strong daughter he knew to give in.

Left with empty arguments, and seeing the possibilities for his daughter, Guang Qian relinquished his misgivings and gave Joshua his reluctant consent.

To Li Li, the swirl of sudden events was like being pulled into the rapids of a river that only moments ago had been tranquil and safe — sweeping her away into something larger than she could comprehend.

From her bedroom where she waited, Li Li could hear the gravity in her father's strained voice. It seemed his discussion with Joshua would never come to an end. When Guang Qian called his youngest daughter back into the room, she knew his answer by the look on Joshua's face. At last, the English teacher received the answer to the prayer he had long feared was an impossible request.

On September 11, 1986, Li Li and Joshua were engaged.

∿

That fall, Joshua sat ramrod straight in a chair in the middle of a small room at the Hun He Hotel, straining to focus on the questions the security officials threw at him like playground bullies throwing punches.

For two weeks, he had started and ended each day praying for the nerve to ask the Public Security Bureau for the passport required to leave China. With great fanfare Deng Xiaoping had invited the Western world into China eight years before, but China made it difficult for its people to obtain the document permitting passage out. And it was unheard of for anyone to leave to study at a religious institution.

Bracing himself for the worst, Joshua rode his bike to the gloomy public security building, a former Japanese police station built during the Sino-Japanese War. He filled out the application for a passport and turned it in. Immediately, the suspicious officials went to work searching for reasons to reject it.

Now he was being hounded at the hotel where he had been ordered to appear. The security officials could not believe he wanted to study at a Bible college. The questions came faster than he could answer them.

"Who is this American sponsor? What is her political affiliation? Where is the money coming from?"

Joshua tried to suppress the rising fear that was screaming at him to flee. Gathering his wits, he tried to keep pace with the questions. He told his interrogators what he thought they wanted to hear, while trying to remain faithful to the truth.

But his answers did not satisfy them.

The following week he was ordered to the security bureau for a second interrogation. A witness to the ugly persecution of the Cultural Revolution that had nearly broken his father, he considered not showing up. But he had come too far to give up. He steeled himself to play David to the communist Goliath.

Again, he was summoned, this time back to the Hun He Hotel. Finally came the question he had been expecting. "Why," one official inquired gruffly, "do you want to study the Bible?"

The English teacher relaxed for a moment and gave the answer — an answer that he had carefully prepared.

"I teach classes on Western civilization," he said. "Mao, our beloved leader, once said the foundation of Western civilization is the Bible. To be a better teacher for our government, I must study that foundation."

His interrogator was silent. He glanced at the other security officials. No one spoke. None wanted to be black-balled for showing ignorance of Mao's wisdom.

The answer to that single question ended the interrogation.

Back at the security bureau, Joshua waited anxiously. Three hours had passed before his name was called. At the security desk, he was finally handed his passport.

On that day, Joshua became the first mainland China student since the communist takeover to be permitted by the government to study at a Bible college in the United States.

Before the officials could change their minds, Joshua rushed to the U.S. Consulate. The smile on the face of the gentlemanly American official was something he knew he would never forget. The official congratulated him. Joshua's visa was the only one he could remember issuing in such a circumstance.

But as one hurdle was cleared, another rose up in front of him. Now Joshua had to find the money to get to America. The airline ticket from Beijing to America cost about four hundred dollars. With a paycheck of seven dollars a month at the University of Fushun, there was no way he could come up with the money. He went to the university, the only place he knew could help. He pleaded with dubious officials to lend him the money. The answer was no. How could he expect them to trust a teacher who skipped his own classes? He offered every argument he could think of. Still they would not budge. Pleading, he told them he had nowhere else to turn. It seemed divine intervention when he finally left the office with a loan for three thousand RMB.

At the money exchange window at the Bank of China, he exchanged his savings for thirty U.S. dollars, the maximum a Chinese citizen was allowed to receive. He gave fifteen dollars of it to Li Li. The rest he hid away in the pocket of the underwear his mother had sewn for him.

He had few belongings to pack, only his clothes, a couple of books, and his Bible. Li Li could not believe it was really happening. Together, the pair boarded a crowded train. On the long trip to the airport in Beijing, she tried not to let him see her crying.

It was in his nation's capital that he encountered his first sign of the Western world he would soon live in. In the restroom, he came upon his first raised, white, porcelain toilet. Until then, the only toilets he'd seen were holes in the ground. He didn't know what to do. He paused, pondering the mysterious plumbing fixture, trying to understand how to proceed. Then, it suddenly became clear to him. He climbed up on the toilet bowl and balanced with one foot perched on each side of the seat, pleased with himself for figuring it out.

In the line to enter customs, Joshua turned to hug his fiancée one last time, his eyes shining with excitement.

"Be careful," she managed to say before finally letting him go. The tears in her eyes seeped down her cheeks.

"I'll write you every day," he promised.

He showed his passport to the customs official and filed through the gate, turning back to flash a confident smile at her. Li Li waved goodbye, watching him disappear. She could hardly fathom that he was gone, and she ached when she realized she had no idea how long it would be before she would see him again.

It was the first commercial flight of his life, and the takeoff of the China Eastern airplane thrilled him. In the air, a flight attendant asked if he wanted a drink. Thirsty, he gratefully took the lukewarm tea she handed him.

Sixteen hours later in San Francisco, he boarded the plane that would take him to Florida to meet his American sponsor. This time, it was an American flight attendant who offered him a drink. But the question she asked left him stymied.

"What would you like: Beer, wine, Coke, Diet Coke, Sprite?"

Not in all his life had anyone given him such a choice. In China, he gratefully took whatever was offered. Joshua was not sure what to do. The attendant repeated the question.

"Coke," he stammered.

Once beaten down by his own government, he sipped his first taste of freedom.

Yi chun guang yin yi chun jin,
chun jin nan mai chun guang yin.

A piece of time is a piece of gold,
but even if you have a piece of gold
you may not be able to buy a piece of time.

FOUR

AMONG THE GIANTS
1987

A distracted Guang Qian stood in front of his youngest daughter amid the clatter of the airport. His mind racing, he glanced furtively over Li Li's shoulder at the uniformed security officers cradling guns in their arms. With a start he realized he was in a restricted area in customs off limits to all but ticketed passengers.

Before the guards could notice him, he turned to Li Li and reminded her once more to write her mother. She smiled back at him, but her confidence did not still the apprehension mounting in his heart. Beneath his calm demeanor, he was afraid something would happen to her.

Looking intently into his daughter's dark brown eyes, he repeated the Confucius saying he had taught her as child:

San si er hou xing.
Think three times before you do anything.

Reassuring himself one last time that he had done all a faithful father could to prepare his daughter for this journey half a world away, he walked off without even saying "I love you." Chinese fathers did not make such declarations to their daughters. As he walked away, he looked back just one time, long enough to see that she was still smiling at him, even though her eyes now seemed blurred in tears. Neither had any idea how long it would be before they would see each other again. Disconsolate, he turned away, shaking his head. Even though he had given his consent, he wondered if this marriage would ever work.

Unlike the father she revered, at twenty-three Li Li felt no fear on this day. The time had come to travel to America to marry her fiancé.

It was Joshua who had encouraged her to take an English name he had found in the Bible. Thumbing through the pages of her dictionary, Li Li came to the English version of her name. Lily was a good name, she thought, although Joshua did not see her as a delicate flower. He knew her well enough to see the power that dwelled beneath her calm surface.

She had persuaded her reluctant superiors at Fushun Law Firm II to authorize a six-month sabbatical to America. She had promised them she would return to her job at the firm, where already she had quadrupled her monthly salary to thirty dollars. It was more than enough for a young Chinese woman who wore uniforms provided by her employer and lived with her parents in a city where lunch cost a few cents and a dress a couple of dollars. She had no idea that her monthly income would barely last a day in America.

Now in her purse she carried sixty U.S. dollars. In her single suitcase were the items her fiancé had instructed her to bring: A Chinese chopping knife, a Chinese-English dictionary, souvenirs, and other gifts of fine silk. She had also packed her formal Chinese silk dresses for summer and her knee-high boots, fur hat, and long coat for the winter.

She spoke no English, but she felt certain that she would pick it up before she returned to China with her husband at year's end. Nowhere in her mind's swirl of confidence was the slightest inkling that this journey would sweep her away from the life she had always known.

Lily blinked both eyes hard, and her feet took root when she stepped out of the crowded airport onto the streets of San Francisco. She had grown accustomed to the new contact lenses that had made her poor vision surprisingly sharp, but she could not believe what she saw.

Not in all her travels as an attorney in China had she seen people so huge and streets so jammed with cars. Nowhere here did she see a single bicycle. Yet it was far quieter than the incessant horn-honking and bell-ringing she was accustomed to on China's streets. Lily was mesmerized, but the strange sights of America made her move closer to her escort, a friend of Joshua's sponsor.

An elderly Chinese man slight in stature, Mr. Chen led Lily past the endless line of automobiles, bumper-to-bumper in the street. Nearly to the crosswalk, she abruptly stopped again, her eyes wide. In front of them was a woman — a very large woman. She was like nothing Lily had ever encountered in China. She seemed to Lily to be a giant, and Lily could only stare. She had no idea that people could be so big. Quickly, Mr. Chen took Lily's elbow, moving her along to avoid any embarrassment.

Riding down the superhighway in Mr. Chen's American-made car was exhilarating. Like most of China's one billion people, Lily's family did not own an automobile. The buses on the roads back home lumbered along at twenty or thirty miles per hour. Now, she could see the speedometer hit seventy as they sailed down the highway to San Jose.

After dinner, the family of the Filipino pastor she stayed with invited her to accompany them to the grocery store. Up for the adventure, Lily was fascinated by the strange new world she had entered. Even the vegetables in the produce aisle were gigantic. Astonished, she picked up a huge bunch of celery with two hands. In China, a stalk of celery was barely bigger than a pencil. Replacing it, she spotted a red bell pepper so big it seemed inflated like a balloon. The red peppers she was used to were the size of lemons.

Suddenly it seemed to make sense: Americans grow big vegetables. Americans eat big vegetables. No wonder they grow to be giants.

She wondered what other fantastical surprises awaited her in South Carolina. It had been six months since she had last seen Joshua. It was hard for her to fathom that in a month she would be his wife.

Her girlfriends from the university had tried to imagine what it would be like to be married in a Western wedding. At the marriage ceremonies they had attended, the bride wore *hong qi pao,* a red silk gown that was the traditional Chinese wedding dress. The ceremonies were held in public restaurants crackling with noisy fireworks. Lily, on the other hand, would say her vows in a solemn ceremony in a quiet church dressed in a white bridal gown.

~

Lily pulled her long, black hair back into a ponytail and admired the new green-striped Western dress Joshua had sent from America. His longing to fit in and his sense of style made him acutely self-conscious of American fashion, and he wanted to share that with Lily.

In the United States, he had carefully explained to her, women changed clothes every day, even if what they wore was not soiled. Lily could not imagine why. At home, she and her friends wore the same set of clothing to work all week. Even stranger to her was Joshua's claim that Americans bathed every day. Growing up, neither Lily nor Joshua had a bathtub or shower in their apartments. Every few weeks Joshua paid a few cents to wash at a public bathhouse in a huge tub with dozens of others. Lily bathed weekly with the families of workers in a tub provided by the company where her mother worked. Already Lily's head was starting to spin as she tried to wrap it around the strange new universe into which she had stepped.

It was five days after she had left her hometown seven thousand miles away that Lily walked into an airport terminal in South Carolina. She scanned the sea of blonds and brunettes until at last she spotted Joshua's black hair. Slowly, she started toward him. In China, even after a long absence, the custom was for loved ones to greet one another formally — a handshake or perhaps a quick embrace. But on this day, Joshua sprinted to Lily and crashed into her, throwing his arms around her and holding her tight.

"Finally," he said, looking into her dancing eyes, "you're here."

When at last he let go, she laughed happily.

For some reason she reached up to her ear. One of her favorite earrings was gone. The force of their embrace must have knocked it loose. For an awkward moment, they both fell to their knees, searching under the seats for the lost earring.

"Never mind," Joshua said, knowing nothing could ruin this joyful day. "We'll buy another one."

Joshua had warned Lily about the heat of America's Deep South, but it had in no way prepared her for the blast of oppressive heat and humidity that slammed into her when they stepped out of the air-conditioned coolness of the airport. By the time she arrived at the home of the daughter of Joshua's sponsor, Lily was sweaty and sticky. Perhaps there was something to this notion of daily baths, she thought. The kind couple welcomed her into their house, where she would be a guest until the wedding.

At breakfast the next morning, Lily came to the table wearing a Chinese silk dress.

"You look like you're going to church," her hostess teased good-heartedly, pointing to her dress.

Blushing, Lily smiled shyly at the family grinning around the kitchen table. Their words were incomprehensible to her, and she didn't quite know why they were laughing.

Later that day inside an American department store, Lily became the owner of her first pair of summer shorts, a gift from her host family.

Wherever Joshua and her hosts took her those first few weeks, Lily carried her pocket dictionary. She greeted people she met by practicing the phrases that Joshua had written out on a card for her. Over and over she struggled to sound out the strange words, determined not to be seen as a fool by people who could not understand her.

"Hello, my name is Lily. I am here to marry Joshua."

Unable to understand anything they said or answer the questions they asked, she was left with nothing more to say. In that painful silence, she lived those first weeks doing what her father had taught her to do when she was uncomfortable.

"If you don't know what to say, what's right or wrong," he told her, "just smile."

As the days passed, smiling wordlessly became increasingly humiliating for her. The English flew out of the mouths of her new friends so fast that she was lost. Uneasy in this new land, she felt timid, afraid to even answer the phone when her host family was away. Soon Lily felt as if she were drowning — utterly helpless in this foreign country. Her only lifeline was Joshua and his ability to bridge the chasm between Mandarin and English.

In the student dormitory at Columbia Bible College, Joshua was a rare oddity — the first mainland Chinese student to attend the college. The English words he had studied so hard to learn did not sound the same here. The Deep South drawl of his fellow students made him feel as if he were hearing a strange new language.

Not only was he frustrated by his inability to understand the students, he was confused by their pranks. The practical jokes they played on the new foreign student were meant to be harmless and funny, but to Joshua they were hurtful. When he attempted to reciprocate, the students did not understand what he was doing, leaving him isolated and frustrated.

One day he was sitting by himself at a table in a classroom building when a middle-aged woman approached him, thrusting out her hand. Surprised, he stood up and shook it. He had no idea who she was or what she wanted. Her name was Liz Layman, and she was a graduate student learning to teach English as a second language.

"May I interview you?" she asked.

His puzzled expression conveyed his doubts.

"It's an assignment for a class I'm taking," she said. "I have to ask a foreign student how he happened to learn English."

It seemed a strange question to him, but he said yes. A pang of warmth deep inside made him realize that it was the first time anyone at the college had cared to hear his story.

The pursuit of English was sparked long ago, when Joshua saw the translator between President Nixon and Chairman Mao. By middle school, he was obsessed with learning the language of Westerners. His English teacher was a widower from Shanghai, and Joshua visited him every day after school to study. At thirteen, he heard that in Shenyang a professor held English lectures every month. His mother borrowed the money for her son to take the train to the capital city of Liaoning an hour away. But when he got there, he didn't know where to go. After a frustrating search, he gave up trying to find the lecture he had traveled so far to hear. On the train home, lost in thoughts on how he would ever manage to learn English, he missed the stop for Fushun. Frightened to find himself in a strange new city, he sat down on a bench and wept. A kind man came to his rescue, helping him find the train back to Fushun. At home, he tried to will away his discouragement. Nothing, he vowed, would stand in his way of learning English. He bought an English dictionary and committed to memorize ten new words each day.

When Deng Xiaoping invited the Western world into China, the study of English became fashionable, and China began broadcasting an hour-long English program each day. Joshua's father's radio was fifteen years old, and the reception was so weak that his son sometimes spent several minutes trying to tune in the right frequency. When finally Joshua found the program, his father shushed the whole family.

"Nobody talk!" he roared. "Joshua is trying to learn English."

In high school, at the house of another English teacher, he studied after school until ten o'clock at night, when he caught the last bus home. In the closet-sized study room his father built, he worked late into the night. His younger sister would find him there after midnight, slumped over his books. His perseverance paid off, and Joshua went on to win several awards in competitions that tested students' ability to write and speak English.

Liz marveled at the outspoken young man's perseverance. His peers saw Joshua as a misfit, but Liz could see that this student whose broken English was hard to understand was not only strong-minded but ambitious. There was no way, she thought, that a man without Joshua's resourcefulness would have been able to get out of China.

Impressed, she invited him home for dinner to meet her husband, Dr. Jack Layman, a professor of American history and Western civilization at the college. Joshua accepted the offer, relishing the idea of spending time in an American home. When he met the rest of Liz's family, Joshua was surprised to see that several of the Layman children were biracial — African and Caucasian.

"They're adopted," Liz said, smiling.

Reading the confusion on his face, she explained that she and her husband were once missionaries in Africa. In the decade they lived in Kenya, they grew attached to the African children at the local orphanage and became foster parents to several orphans. Back home in America, after raising their four biological daughters, they adopted four children.

It all seemed natural to Liz. But to Joshua, adoption was unheard of. He knew it went on in secret in China, but rarely was it acknowledged or discussed. Admitting that a son or daughter had been adopted was considered shameful, and no one wanted to risk losing face by revealing that their children were not their own biological offspring.

"God's family is our family," Liz told him. "And our house is the Lord's house."

As missionaries, the Laymans were all too familiar with the extreme loneliness suffered by foreigners living in a strange place. When the holiday break came and the students emptied out of the dormitories, Joshua was left alone. The Laymans invited him to stay in their basement, and the guest room became his second home. It leaked when it rained, but he barely noticed. He cared only that these new friends who understood him had stepped into his isolated life.

On July 11, 1987, one day before her twenty-fourth birthday, Lily Nie married Joshua Zhong at Cornerstone Presbyterian Church.

Joshua was the only one in the entire church that Lily had known for more than a month. Seated in the pews were nearly four hundred church members, college teachers, and students who had been invited to the wedding and reception — both gifts from Joshua's American sponsor.

When Lily saw the packed church and heard the organist play the first notes of the traditional wedding march, a wave of emotion rushed over her. She had heard the famous music before but never expected it to be played for her in a church filled with strangers. She walked down the aisle in pure white.

The sight of her overwhelmed Joshua. The woman he had pursued so long was entrancing, even though the long wedding gown she wore was second-hand and pinned to fit. He winced at the thought, regretting he was unable to buy her a wedding dress of her own. In that moment, he felt at once like both a beggar and a king.

"We are here today to unite this woman and this man in holy matrimony," the minister said. "Today Joshua and Lily proclaim their love to the world …"

Joshua felt the immense power of the words and the utter powerlessness of a man dependent on others for everything. He reminded himself what was most important. He must make sure that Lily understood the vows she was making. As the minister recited them, Joshua repeated the words to Lily in Chinese.

Lily responded in a voice so soft that few of the people in the pews could hear her. But it did not matter. Lily and Joshua were, against all odds, husband and wife.

Lily and Joshua began their new life together very much in love, but very much without. The newlyweds' home was a student-housing trailer that their sponsor leased for them. To furnish it, Joshua made many shopping trips — to the college storage room, scavenging through cast-off furniture that the school had squirreled away. He hauled home a mattress, a couch, and a table. The only new things in their trailer were the cooking utensils, tableware, blankets, and laundry baskets the wedding guests had given them. On one wall, they taped the hundreds of wedding cards they'd received into the shape of a cross. As they settled into their first home, they began at last to feel a sense of belonging together.

Joshua's friends the Laymans thought his seemingly shy new wife was lovely and sweet. They had no idea of the iron will hidden inside the young woman who seemed to be reeling in culture shock. Seeing Lily's difficulty with the language, Liz offered to teach her English. On Tuesdays and Thursdays, Lily made the fifteen-minute walk to the Layman home. In large print on index cards, Liz wrote out responses to common questions. For hours Lily practiced the simple sentences.

"I am married to Joshua. He is a student at the Bible college."

As part of Lily's English lessons that summer, Liz read to her from the Bible. Lily had been curious about the strange Bible stories ever since Joshua had started reading them to her in China.

"You should go to women's Bible study," Liz suggested. "You could learn the Bible and practice English too."

Lily agreed to go, even though she knew she would understand little of what was said. Before summer turned to autumn, the young Chinese woman who had grown up knowing nothing about Jesus was baptized at Cornerstone Presbyterian Church. As she struggled to cope with the massive changes in her life, she found herself increasingly seeking comfort in her new-found faith. On the days she seemed to be sinking in shifting sands, she relished the grounded feeling her faith provided.

In September, it was time for Joshua to return to his classes at the college. Stripped of Joshua's outgoing personality, their stark trailer grew starker, and Lily's new life felt shallow and empty. She was homesick for China and for her family. Their trailer had no telephone, but once a month she borrowed a neighbor's to call home.

"America is wonderful," she told her parents, trying to sound cheerful. "I love it."

She didn't want to lie, but she wouldn't ever worry them by telling the truth about the loneliness that filled her.

"I miss you," she would tell them, but always with a lightness in her voice that belied her heavy heart.

At home, she had been able to talk with her mother about anything, and she yearned for the happy days and late nights laughing and talking with her girlfriends. She longed to taste the familiar, comforting foods of China. She could almost taste her mother's tiger-skin eggs — hard boiled and dropped into oil, then fried until the skin was curly and golden. She yearned to be in her homeland, secure and rooted among family and friends. Here she simply felt lost.

Most of all, she missed waking each morning and going to work. At her law firm, she used everything she had learned to help her business clients run their companies. At home, neighbors had come knocking at the door of her family's apartment, asking for help from attorney Nie. No day was wasted. She had lived by the Confucius saying:

Yi chun guang yin yi chun jin, chun jin nan mai chun guang yin.

A piece of time is a piece of gold, but even if you have a piece of gold you may not be able to buy a piece of time.

Now the long autumn days alone in their trailer seemed meaningless. She washed their laundry, scrubbed the trailer clean, and taught herself to cook. But mostly, she waited for Joshua to come home.

One warm day, she no longer could bear being inside the trailer. While watering their dry lawn, she gazed up the hill at the hardwoods abandoning their summer greens for flaming red. In an instant, her truth struck her with the force of an earthquake.

I am nobody. I'm useless.

She turned off the water, walked into the trailer, sat down, and cried.

Here in the United States, she was of no value to anyone. People were kind to her, but they treated her like a helpless baby, telling her what to eat and how to use the most basic things. They started a conversation then left her out, assuming she didn't understand. When they wanted to ask her a question, they turned to Joshua. It was as if she knew nothing.

She had worked hard to learn English. In the mornings, jogging along a trail near their house, she boldly stopped the people who said good morning.

"Can you teach me a sentence of English?"

If they offered a sentence she already knew, she asked for another. At college gatherings and church meetings, she practiced. At home, she tried to be useful. She offered to help Joshua with his schoolwork, and he salvaged a typewriter for her from the used-equipment room at school. She tried to type his papers, but she found it impossible to read his scrawl.

The invitation to come to America and marry Joshua had been filled with promise. Now broken, she felt like a failure. In despair, one night she told him the truth that she had been hiding.

"I want to go home."

Joshua watched his new wife silently cooking at the stove. Her misery seemed to fill the room. At the time he thought he'd be happiest, he felt miserably helpless. There was no money now for an airline ticket back to China. They were depending on his sponsor to purchase their airline tickets home at year's end. To return any sooner was not possible. Their living expenses devoured the meager three-dollars-per-hour paycheck he received for washing dishes in the college cafeteria. But Lily was desperate to be in control of her own being.

"I'll go to work," Lily said.

"Doing what?" Joshua asked. "Who will hire someone who can't speak English?"

"I don't know," she said. "But I'll find something."

That fall the attorney from China became a maid in America. On her hands and knees, she scrubbed the toilets and tubs of strangers, trying desperately to push away the persistent question, "What would my mother think if she could see me?"

By day Lily cleaned houses, and at night she became a babysitter, even though she had no idea what to do. She'd had no younger siblings; she'd never even wished for one. The few babies in her army apartment building were of no interest. She'd never even held one. Her older sister had a baby boy and Lily had fed him, but he bit her once, so she left him alone.

The first time she tried to change a diaper, she cringed.

I'm not even a mother. And here I am changing the dirty diapers of a stranger's child.

To save money, Lily and Joshua wore the secondhand clothes that neighbors dropped off at the couple's trailer. The two of them lived on one boiled chicken a week. Still, there was not enough for a four hundred dollar ticket to China.

She ached to go home now, but she reassured herself that they would return together by year's end. Even as she scrubbed toilets and changed diapers, it was the single hope that she held fast in her heart, the thing that kept her grounded. Soon she would be back in China.

But one night as they lay in bed, Joshua blindsided her.

"Lily, I'm staying in America," he said quietly.

"What do you mean?" she asked, gaping.

"I can't go back now. I've been here a year and have nothing to show for it. I have to get a degree."

To return to his family and Lily's parents without one would mean losing face. Lily's father still looked down on him, and Joshua's own father had high expectations for his bright son in America. Joshua desperately wanted to prove himself. He had signed a statement swearing to return to China after his scholarship ended, but he no longer saw any future there.

"I'm going to seminary," he said.

In the depth of her gut, Lily could feel the earth drop from beneath her.

Joshua had already inquired about scholarships at Denver Seminary in Colorado and Trinity Evangelical Divinity School in Illinois. To his surprise, both were eager to obtain their first mainland Chinese student. When he learned that Dr. Ralph Covell, the dean of Denver Seminary, had served as a missionary in China for twenty years and spoke fluent Mandarin, Joshua knew where he would go. What he did not know was whether his homesick wife would agree to go with him.

But Lily's reaction was not the only wild card. When his sponsor learned about Joshua's scholarship, she was livid. It had long been her intent to bring the new Christian believer to Columbia Bible College for one year of training so he could return to his homeland and evangelize. When Joshua refused her demand that he go back to China, his loyal sponsor turned adversary.

Furious that the young man had defied her, she withdrew her sponsorship and informed Columbia Bible College that she had cut him off. She called Denver Seminary and claimed the Chinese student was no longer welcome at Columbia and should be sent back to China.

Before long Joshua realized he had trouble on two fronts: His sponsor was pressuring Denver Seminary to rescind his scholarship, and Columbia was challenging his motives for study.

All of the Layman children were asleep and Jack Layman was at his desk preparing for the next day's class when the doorbell's ring pierced the quiet, autumn evening. Before he could reach the front entrance, the bell rang out a second time. He opened the door to Joshua's frantic face.

"I have to talk to you," the young man said, his eyes filled with panic.

Dr. Layman could see that something was terribly wrong. He showed the distressed student to a chair at the kitchen table.

"What is it?" he asked, unable to imagine what could have terrified his young Chinese friend.

Trembling, Joshua told the professor that he had been ordered to a meeting at the college. Behind closed doors, he had been questioned, scolded, and shamed.

"They're trying to get my scholarship withdrawn," Joshua said, breaking down. "They accused me of being a communist spy!"

Dr. Layman wrapped his arm around the shoulder of the young man he had come to think of as a son, calmly reassuring Joshua that he would stand by him. Inside, the professor was incensed at the way this foreign student had been treated.

The following day on the campus he sought out Joshua's teachers and interviewed them. They confirmed that the young man was in good standing. Next, he met with both the dean and the president of Columbia Bible College. Neither knew about the accusations. Jack Layman made a long-distance call to the dean of Denver Seminary. There was absolutely no merit, he reported, to the claim that the Chinese student had been dismissed from Columbia.

To his relief, Joshua learned his seminary scholarship was safe. But with his American sponsorship withdrawn, the young couple were in danger of deportation. Being forced back to China now would be devastating to Joshua — far worse than simply returning without a degree.

Again, Jack and Liz Layman came to the couple's rescue, this time agreeing to be Joshua's new sponsor. Jack rushed off a new I-20 immigration form and sponsorship letter to the U.S. Immigration Bureau, successfully allowing the couple to stay in America.

The Laymans loyally stood by them, treating them like family and inviting Lily and Joshua to consider them their American mom and dad. Still, their sponsor's withdrawal of support left Joshua and Lily staggering.

Lily had ridden the frightening roller coaster with Joshua, calming his frayed nerves as he nearly drowned in panic. She knew he badly wanted her to go with him to Denver, but she longed to return home to the family and career she so desperately missed. From her earnings as a maid and babysitter, she had saved nearly enough to buy a plane ticket. She reasoned that it was common in China for couples to be separated, often spending long stretches apart to study or serve in the army. But she worried whether it was safe for Joshua to drive fifteen hundred miles across the country alone. Even if he could raise the money needed for the trip, she doubted their hand-me-down 1964 Chevy Impala could make it.

Then, the unbelievable began to happen. First came a four-thousand-dollar contribution from a seminary student and his wife who had recently sold their house in California and wanted to help. Next, a student leaving the country on a mission trip offered to sell them her 1978 Mercury Zephyr — for just one dollar.

Still, Lily was torn, unable to sort out the thoughts clashing in her mind. In her heart, she knew that leaving her husband when he needed her was unthinkable. Unexpectedly one day, she received the clarity she was searching for. A friend told her about an institute in Denver that taught foreigners English as a second language. It was the encouragement she needed, the missing piece. Her family would expect her to have mastered English when she returned to China. She would go with Joshua and enroll in the Spring International Language Institute.

The battle that had raged in her mind and heart now quelled. Once again she would trust Joshua and leap into the unknown.

On Christmas Day, the young couple sorrowfully said goodbye to the couple they now called Mom and Dad. In the old Mercury Zephyr, they left the Laymans and set off for the West. Lily wondered how they would even make it that first night to Nashville. It had been several months since Joshua had obtained his first driver's license, and already he'd had his first accident. It happened on the highway on the way back from a house Lily had been hired to clean. She was studying the map of downtown Columbia, trying to give Joshua directions. They were arguing about the best way to go when he lost control of the car he'd borrowed. Before he could regain control, they slammed into the center median. Sore necks were all that they suffered, but the cost to repair the damage was several hundred dollars that they could not afford.

After the first leg of their journey they slept in Nashville, where a friend of the Laymans had arranged for them to stay in an empty college dorm room. In St. Louis they spent the night in the home of a Chinese pastor, and in Kansas City they slept in the house of an architect who was the father of a schoolmate. It was in the small town of Hays, Kansas, that their luck ran out. The Zephyr broke down, and they had no choice but to pay for a cheap motel while they waited for the mechanics to fix it.

Five days and eight states after their Columbia departure, Joshua and Lily arrived in Denver — during a huge snowstorm. Driving along Interstate 25, the blowing snow made it hard to see the road. The wipers couldn't work fast enough to reopen the white curtain falling on the windshield. Slammed by the high altitude and freezing temperatures, the car would go no faster than thirty miles per hour. When at last they pulled into a parking lot at Denver Seminary, the one-dollar Mercury Zephyr died.

Once again, there was someone watching out for the young couple. This time it was Dr. Covell, the dean of the school, who came to their rescue. He led the exhausted young couple into the college storage room, where they dug out a used mattress, a few cooking utensils, and some canned food. That night, in Room 110 of married housing, Joshua and Lily slept together on the mattress on the floor.

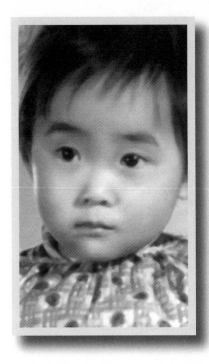

Lily at age three

Lily, five

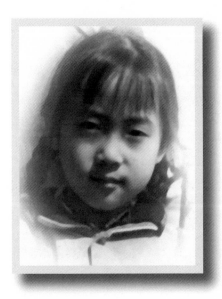

Lily, seven, in Guilin

Lily, eight, singing a
famous song in Guilin

Lily wearing her Little Red
Guard scarf at age eleven

Lily, fourteen

Lily, age eighteen, and the poem she later wrote to Joshua:
"To build an everlasting relationship like the fresh river and
the mountain that follow each other forever, we must have
time to examine each other's hearts."

Lily at high school graduation,
age eighteen

Joshua at age twelve

Liang Zhen with Luo Rui Fen,
Mr. Gu's mother; around 1949

Lily's mother, Liang Zhen, in
military uniform; around 1950

Lily's parents, Liang Zhen and
Guang Qian; late 1950s

Lily's father, Guang Qian; 1963

Lily, three, with her mother and
her doll by the grape vines in
their Yingkou yard; 1966

Lily, six, with her father
on Tiananmen Square; 1969

Lily's parents with
Lao Lao, Grandma Qin; 1999

Lily in her room with the calligraphy
that Joshua made; 1985

Lily, twenty-two, during a bike trip
with Joshua and friends; 1986

Joshua and Lily at the airport before Joshua
leaves for the U.S. for the first time; 1986

Joshua and Lily's wedding in
Columbia, South Carolina; 1987

The birth of
Art and Amy; 1989

Lily with Amy and Art; 1993

Amy and Art, six, with Joshua's
parents, Wei Quan and Wang
Kun; 1996

Ren mei you chi bu liao de ku,
ye mei you xiang bu liao de fu.

There is no hardship a human cannot bear,
no blessing she cannot enjoy.

FIVE

FEED THE BOY FIRST
1989

Lily took a deep breath and went back to scrubbing the white, porcelain tub in the master bathroom in the southeast suburban Denver home where she was a maid. It was the third bathroom she had cleaned that spring afternoon, and she would wash down a dozen more before the day was done. Dropping the sponge, she pressed her hand to her churning stomach. The fumes from the cleaning fluid were overpowering, especially on top of her fatigue. She had gotten only four hours of sleep the night before.

Cleaning houses was one of the five jobs she was working to earn her tuition to the Spring International Language Institute — and she was grateful to have them. Before she went to class at nine o'clock in the morning, she taught Mandarin to a retired couple preparing for a mission trip to Taiwan. Two afternoons a week after school, she cleaned houses.

By seven in the evening, Lily and Joshua were working side by side at the night job Dr. Covell had arranged for them at Denver Seminary. They cleaned seven buildings, emptying trash cans, vacuuming the long hallways, and washing down the bathrooms. Just before midnight, Lily sat down at a desk in the bedroom to start her homework. By two o'clock, she fell into bed.

On weekends, she rode the bus downtown to sell souvenirs at a gift shop during the day and to wait tables at the China Palace restaurant at night. She was tired, but she did not complain. Her mother had shown her how to endure a life working around the clock, and during the long days Lily often silently echoed the proverb her mother had taught her:

> *Ren mei you chi bu liao de ku,*
> *ye mei you xiang bu liao de fu.*
> There is no hardship a human cannot bear,
> no blessing she cannot enjoy.

On Sundays the couple went to Denver Chinese Evangelical Church, where Dr. Covell had invited them to worship. Some days, with great patience and kindness, his wife, Ruth, would help Lily with her English.

The Covells were drawn to the struggling newlyweds who seemed so lost in Denver. Ralph and Ruth had met and married in China, where they both served as missionaries for more than two decades. They'd come to love the Chinese people and understand the ways of their ancient culture. After the young Chinese couple arrived at the seminary, the Covells took them in, finding little ways to help them adapt to life in America. Joshua and Lily were grateful that this caring couple had stepped into their lives, and it was a welcome bonus that the Covells knew Mandarin.

One warm March morning when the daffodils were bringing new life to Denver's dormant gardens, Lily and Joshua were leaving the church sanctuary to go to choir rehearsal. Suddenly Lily grabbed Joshua's arm to keep from falling.

"What's wrong?" he asked, steadying her.

"I have to go home," she said, still swaying from dizziness. There was no way she could make it to choir.

At the basement apartment they rented, Lily walked into the door and collapsed in a heap on the floor. Joshua's first thought was that she had fainted from exhaustion.

When her eyes fluttered open, Joshua insisted that she go to the emergency room, even though she insisted that nothing was wrong. Her insides were swirling, but a jittery stomach was something she'd grown accustomed to during her train trips to call on clients across China.

In the emergency room, the solemn doctor ordered a battery of tests. Soon he returned, smiling.

"Congratulations," he said. "You are not sick. You're pregnant."

Shocked, Lily's eyes welled up, and her mind raced.

I can't be pregnant. I'm not ready to be a mother. I have to work and go to school.

Joshua's initial surprise at the news quickly melted into panic. There was no health insurance to pay for doctor visits, not to mention the delivery room. Unsure what to do, Joshua called on the only person he could turn to for help.

Dr. Covell suggested Lily call for an appointment at the Inner City Clinic, where Ruth volunteered as a nurse. For twenty dollars, she could get checkups from doctors who gave their time as a ministry.

At her first visit, the doctor examined Lily and then slowly shook his head.

"It's not right," he said. "Something's not normal."

The doctor suggested an ultrasound, but that would cost more than a hundred dollars, and there was no way the couple could afford it. Lily wasn't worried. She didn't have time to waste fretting about things she could do nothing about. But Joshua was desperate to find a way to pay for the test.

Several weeks passed and still Joshua could not come up with the money. One day a friend handed him an ad from the school directory. Joshua could not believe the words he read: "The office of Dr. John Heavrin — Denver Seminary students free."

The day of her ultrasound, Lily lay on the exam table as the doctor studied the computer screen.

"God has blessed you so much," he told Lily, "maybe too much."

"What's wrong with me?"

"Nothing," he said, smiling. "You're having twins."

Oh, Lord. I'm not ready for one, and now you give me two.

Lily and Joshua were stunned. And again Lily wept in fear. How could she possibly work, go to school, and care for two newborns? With a start she realized that returning home to China would be even more difficult now.

As she dressed, she prayed, and by the time she left the doctor's office, her fears were melting away. In their place she felt a growing sense of calm, a certainty that God would help her.

Too sick to eat, she slipped from ninety-six pounds to ninety-four as she struggled to finish the paralegal classes she had started. Something had to give.

The day she threw up while she scrubbed a client's tub, she quit her job as a maid.

Days later at the gift shop, she'd just finished ringing up a customer's purchase when she lost what little was in her stomach.

"Don't come back," said her supervisor, her eyes concerned. "It's too hard."

Joshua knew there was no way they could afford to lose Lily's income now. On Friday night, he showed up to take her place at the Chinese restaurant. In one miserable shift of mixed up orders, Joshua failed as a waiter. That Saturday at the gift shop, he quit after a single day of struggling to make change.

At home, Lily was so sick she could do nothing but lie in bed and watch TV, something she had never before had time to do. Amid the seemingly endless stream of American TV, she found her homeland — live on the news from Beijing. Thousands of protesting students were in a standoff with soldiers and army tanks in Tiananmen Square. Shaken by the scene, Lily was both frightened and exhilarated to see her young countrymen so brave and out of control in the face of the communist juggernaut. From the bed day after day, she watched the drama unfold until one morning the newsflash came. Overnight, hundreds of students had been massacred, mowed down by their own government's troops. In horror, the dream she held deep inside also became a casualty.

I can never live in China again.

It was no longer safe for her to raise a family in the country that had been her home. On that sorrowful June fourth, Lily let go of her dream to return to her homeland, her career, and her family. The old life she'd hoped to someday resume in China was gone.

~

At 3:33 p.m. on a cold afternoon after Thanksgiving Day, Joshua's father finally got what neither of his other two sons had been able to give him: a boy. Six minutes later came a girl. It was November 29 in America, November 30 in China.

Long feng tai.
A dragon and a phoenix born the same time.

Such a rare double birth was considered very lucky in China. The odds of having twins were far lower among Asians than Americans, and the chances of a boy and a girl even slimmer.

Joshua phoned Fushun to proudly announce the birth of Art Wei and Amy Nie. To honor their homeland, they also gave each child a Chinese first name: Hua for their son and Xia for their daughter. Together the words Hua Xia mean China.

Now Joshua knew his father could die at peace. A grandson had preserved the Zhong family name.

Ecstatic, Joshua's mother demanded at once to speak to her daughter-in-law.

"Make sure," she declared firmly, "that you feed the boy first."

Lily was speechless. In China, a mother-in-law was powerful, and a daughter-in-law must listen to what she said. Slowly, Lily recovered her voice.

"Yes," she replied, straining to sound respectful. "I will feed them both."

Dialing again to Fushun, they called Lily's parents to announce the news.

"But how are you?" her mother insisted.

"I'm fine, Mama," Lily said.

In truth, Lily was weak with fever and her wrists had been severely strained while bearing down during the difficult double birth. Through the long, painful hours of labor, Ruth Covell never left Lily, hovering over her. When Lily didn't think she could stand it one more minute, Ruth whispered words of encouragement to her.

The day after the delivery, Lily had no strength. The nurses helped the new mother up to walk, but she fainted to the floor, breaking her eyeglasses in two. When they brought her babies to her, Lily's wrists were so badly damaged she could not use her hands to lift them. She braced her forearms tightly around the torsos, and although they were barely six pounds each, it was a strain for her to lift them.

At home, the couple's life seemed to be approaching chaos. The day Joshua opened the hospital bill, he was crushed.

How can they expect me to come up with fourteen thousand dollars?

By then, Joshua had graduated from Denver Seminary, earning the degree he had so long coveted. But for a young man obsessed with finding a better life, it was not enough. He was now studying for a joint doctorate at the University of Denver and Iliff School of Theology on a scholarship secured with the help of Dr. Covell. He earned a small salary working part time at International Students Inc., helping Chinese students stranded in America after the massacre at Tiananmen Square.

Fourteen thousand dollars was more than the average worker in China would make in a lifetime. Joshua could think of nothing to do but to appeal to the hospital officials. Using the persuasive powers that had gotten him this far, Joshua convinced them to cut the bill to seven thousand dollars. Even then, he had no idea how he would pay it. That year, he fed his family of four on food stamps.

It was Ruth Covell who helped Lily survive the first frantic month of motherhood. She arranged for the women at the seminary to visit each day to help with the twins, and she made the new mother the homemade dumpling soup that Lily loved. The Chinese believed the more soup a new mother drank, the more milk she made. Chinese tradition also said that women must not take a bath, brush their teeth, or leave the house for one month after childbirth, or they would have health troubles in old age. If they brushed too soon, their teeth would fall out. If they bathed, they would develop arthritis.

Lily was far too busy to mess with tradition. Her first month was consumed with feedings — at least ten bottles a day — and changing diapers, to the tune of a dozen a day. On Thursdays, Ruth faithfully arrived with home-cooked meals and sacks of groceries, and she insisted on taking home baskets of laundry to wash.

As a mother, Lily grew keenly aware that her babies' lives were in orbit around hers, relying entirely on her. She knew that she was immediately intertwined with the very air they breathed. Several times each night, she would awake with a start. Sometimes it was the cries of hunger or distress that snapped her from sleep. Other nights, it was the stillness that stirred her to her feet. Silently, she would lean over the crib and place a hand on each tiny chest, reassuring herself that her babies were still breathing.

Each time Ruth returned from visiting Lily and the twins, she told her husband how worried she was about the little family that felt like her own.

"They're poor as church mice," Dr. Covell said, sighing. "With two new mouths to feed, I don't know how they'll make it."

But once again, whether through determination, ingenuity, luck, or faith — or a little of each — Lily and Joshua continued to build a life that somehow made living in this strange land worth the pain and effort.

Love brings all of us together.

SIX

FORGOTTEN LIVES
1992

L ily stood in the darkness between two cribs in the tiny house at the foot of the Rocky Mountains. Her long black hair swept across the smooth skin of her oval face as she bent over her sleeping daughter and son. In the halo of the night light, their black lashes rested in half moons on their peaceful faces.

She leaned in to kiss them, breathing in their fresh powder smell. It was what she had done every night since she had brought them into the world two and a half years earlier. She lingered over them. Soon, she would not be able to touch them before she went to bed. She was on the verge of a two week trip, thousands of miles away in China to try to launch a fledgling software company. It would be the first time she had returned to China — and the first time she'd ever left her children.

It was April, and a spring snowstorm sent a wet chill through the Colorado night air. Lily left the soft breathing of her children behind, content that they were warm and dry. Soundlessly, she moved into the kitchen of the house she and Joshua had managed to purchase after five years of scrimping to save enough for a small down payment. On the table, she laid a bag of textbooks and her English pocket dictionary, the pages worn and curled at the corners.

She sat down at the kitchen table where she and her mother had spent so many nights visiting after Lily returned home from the university. Desperate to be with her daughter after the birth of the twins, Liang Zhen had applied ten times for a visa to America. Ten times she was rejected. The babies were fifteen months old and walking when the American Consulate finally agreed to let her go. For the past year, she had cared for her young grandson and granddaughter while Lily finished her human resources degree at Colorado Christian University. Liang Zhen loved her grandbabies, but what she wanted badly was to do something to help her daughter get a good job.

"Women hold up half the sky," she had scolded. Nearly sixteen years after Mao's death, the communist dictator was still revered by China's older generation, even though his cruel policies would be blamed by some historians for the deaths of tens of millions of his people. Despite the havoc he had wreaked, Mao's faithful followers believed he had pushed the country forward in many ways, including his effort to change a culture that had favored males over females for five thousand years.

Liang Zhen's desire for Lily to work did not go unnoticed. Lily still could feel the disappointment from her childhood, when she caused her mother to lose face by failing the medical school entrance examination in China. She did not want to let her down again.

In Denver, Lily had learned English at the international language institute and earned a bachelor's degree. Still, no matter how many times she interviewed, she could not find a job that paid much better than what she'd earned cleaning toilets and waiting tables. The few times she was offered an entry-level clerical job, her husband flatly told her no.

"You're too smart, Lily," he said, adamant. "I know you can do better."

Liang Zhen was not so patient. As a young mother of two, she'd worked round the clock during Mao's relentless drive to industrialize China. She was an independent woman, determined to contribute her fair share to the household income, and she expected the same from her own daughters. Some evenings at the kitchen table, Liang Zhen would go on symbolic hunger strikes to show her disapproval of her youngest daughter who brought home no paycheck.

"Mama, you must eat," Lily pleaded.

"How can I take food provided by my son-in-law with no help from my daughter?" her mother protested.

Liang Zhen finally rediscovered her appetite after Lily enrolled in graduate school, assured by her son-in-law that a master's degree in business administration would bring her daughter an important job in America.

As a class project to develop their entrepreneurial skills, Lily and several students had formed a software company. Their idea was to hire cheap labor in China to do computer programming for Colorado banks. Lily was named international vice president, a position that sounded promising to Liang Zhen. But before Lily was anywhere near earning a paycheck, her mother's one-year visa expired. Now the house seemed quiet without her.

Lily switched on the light and slipped into bed. She looked into the face of her sleeping husband. It was rare to see him at rest. Joshua was a man who could not keep his head down. He was always looking up and looking out. His forward-thinking mind was forever thrust into the future, propelled by a visionary drive unknown to many men in China whose focus was to survive each day.

On their bedside table that cold spring night was a stack of books and papers. No matter how tired she was, Lily had made it a habit to read before she fell asleep. From the bottom of the pile she pulled a folded newspaper. It was a February issue of China's *People's Daily*. Joshua had spotted it in the dorm room of a friend. He brought it home, insisting that she read an article announcing the implementation of a new law. Now, two months had passed.

"You're always saying you need to keep up with China's laws," he had told her.

"I know," she said, feeling that same old pang of desire, wishing again she could one day return to her law practice. But she knew her husband had no intention of ever living in China again.

She pulled out the *People's Daily* and opened it. On page three, she spotted the headline:

Adoption Law of the People's Republic of China

Scanning the Chinese characters, she read through the new law until she came to the words that stopped her:

Foreigners can adopt children from China.

She finished reading the article and reached over to turn out the light. Most nights, sleep came easily. But that night Lily lay wide awake, thinking back to the day six years earlier when she had stumbled into the orphanage in her home town. There in the darkness, the sounds and smells were vivid. She could see the hopeless eyes, the dirty faces of the abandoned children who lived there. Now her homeland was facing the escalating crisis in its overcrowded orphanages and opening adoption to foreigners in hopes of finding homes for abandoned children whose numbers had grown to hundreds of thousands.

Into Lily's mind came Jack and Liz Layman, the only adoptive parents she knew.

Lily and Joshua ate breakfast at the kitchen table while the twins nibbled Cheerios from the trays of their highchairs.

"I read about the new law in the *People's Daily*," she said slowly.

"What did you think?"

"Maybe we could get a Chinese girl for the Laymans," she said quietly.

"The Laymans?" Joshua said, grinning. "They're in their sixties!"

By the time the breakfast dishes were cleared, the *People's Daily* story was forgotten.

Lily had only a few weeks to prepare for the long journey she was about to take. For years she had thought constantly about China, and finally the day was coming when she would return. She remembered that long ago day in the office of Fushun Law Firm II when she had solemnly promised her superiors she would be home in just six months. Now she was filled with excitement — she would see her father for the first time since he had walked away in the crowded airport. It had been five years.

But family was not the main purpose of her trip. She was going back to her homeland to attempt to negotiate a joint venture between her startup company and a China firm. It meant leaving her small children behind for two weeks, something Lily had been dreading for months. But if she succeeded with the joint venture, it could be the beginning of the new career that she had worked so hard for.

A few days before her departure, she received an unexpected phone call from China. It was a woman she knew from International Students Inc. who was teaching English in Nanjing.

"Lily, I want to adopt a baby before I come home."

"That's wonderful," Lily said. "I just read about the new law."

"You're a lawyer. What should I do?"

"Go to the Civil Affairs Bureau and register," Lily told her. "If you have any trouble, call me."

She hung up, thinking it a strange coincidence. It was the second time in a month that China's new adoption law had wound its way into her life.

Lily watched the bright lights of Shanghai slowly disappear below her as the plane headed back home to America over the dark nothingness of the Pacific Ocean. Even as the plane climbed, she felt a sinking disappointment — the opposite of the high hopes she'd arrived with nearly two weeks earlier.

Returning to her homeland had sent her head swirling. Hundreds of new high-rises soared into the sophisticated Shanghai skyline, and a steady stream of automobiles edged out the bicycles on the crowded streets. The last time she'd been in the city as an attorney for Fushun Law Firm II, her hotel room cost just five dollars. The hundred-dollar tab she received for one night's stay this visit left her gasping for air. It was more than her first year's salary at the law firm. Never at age twenty-three could she have imagined the drastic change that would take place in this city known as China's crown jewel.

From Shanghai she'd flown to Shenyang, the capital city of Liaoning near her hometown. As she stepped off the plane in her home province, she saw her father — the man she remembered as always unflappable, always so dignified — hopping up and down frantically, trying to spot his daughter in the sea of passengers. Seeing her, he cried: "Li Li!" Hearing him call out her name again sent waves of electricity through her. Guang Qian pushed his way through the crowd and threw his arms around his youngest daughter, now twenty-eight years old. With his daughter finally home again, his joy and relief left him weeping.

It was his idea for Lily to come to China to attend a huge business conference in Fushun. He saw it as her best chance to jumpstart the business she was trying to get off the ground. In her phone calls with him, the possibility of partnering with the company where her sister, Ke Ke, worked seemed promising. But after several days of talks, the deal Lily had traveled halfway around the world to negotiate fell apart.

Leaning back in her seat on the plane, she reached into her purse and retrieved a picture of Art and Amy, their faces illuminated by the small overhead light. One more day and she wouldn't have to settle for gazing at their picture. She'd be holding them close. She had not realized how deeply she could ache for them. She slid her seat all the way back and closed her eyes, remembering her initial panic when she learned she would be having twins. Now, every fiber of her being seemed to confirm quite the opposite: She'd be content if she never had to leave her children again.

Lily rubbed her eyes and blinked, staring again into the computer screen at the school library. It was May, and all that sunny spring morning she'd been sitting at a desk, researching a term paper for business school. It was time to pack up her things. Joshua and the twins would be waiting for her to come home for lunch.

Just one more search.

From deep beneath the surface of her consciousness floated one word: adoption. Without thinking, she typed it in. Instantly, hundreds of citations flashed up. She narrowed her search, adding the word international. A shorter list appeared, and she scanned it, still not finding what she was looking for. Her fingers tapped out: China adoption. This time, just two entries popped up. She opened them, clicked print, grabbed the articles off the printer, and headed home.

When she walked into the door, she set her things down and strolled into the kitchen. There, laid out on the kitchen table, were two computer printouts. Two words leaped off the page at her: China adoption.

"What are these?" she called out to Joshua.

"I found them today," he said, walking into the kitchen.

He had been unable to shake the idea of adoption from his mind. He wondered if it was the memory of his mother's own painful adoption that had driven him to the computer. Wang Kun had not told him she had been adopted until he was in college, fearing it somehow made her less worthy and would bring shame to her son.

"Wait," Lily said, turning and leaving the room.

In seconds she returned, carrying her book bag. From inside it, she pulled out the same two articles and handed them to her husband.

All they could do was stare at each other.

On one side of the family room, Guang Qian and Liang Zhen chattered in rapid-fire Mandarin, gesturing dramatically to make a point. On the other, Jack and Liz Layman responded with equal enthusiasm in English. Back and forth, Joshua and Lily translated English into Mandarin for their Chinese parents, then Mandarin into English for their American mom and dad.

In the heat of Colorado's dry summer, Lily's parents had flown in from Fushun so that Guang Qian could finally meet his grandchildren. Jack Layman and his wife had come to visit from South Carolina. The two men from opposite sides of the world took an instant liking to one another, quickly finding something they agreed on: "There is no true wisdom until you reach sixty."

Lily had refrained from bringing up Chinese adoption to her parents, knowing it was not a topic that was spoken about in China. But Joshua could not wait to find out what the Laymans thought of the new law.

"We read about China opening adoption to foreigners. Do you think Americans would be willing to adopt Chinese children?"

"I think you'd be surprised," Liz answered without hesitation. "A lot of couples would love the chance. I think they'd jump at the opportunity."

Lily was heartened by the response. "Maybe we could help."

"Of course you could — you'd be perfect," Liz said. "You should try."

Lily translated for her father, and immediately he shook his head and walked away.

Bethany Christian Services was the agency that the Laymans recommended, and first thing Monday morning Joshua was on the phone. Once he got an idea, he could not shake it from his head until he acted on it. Lily had not yet given up on her software company, but Joshua saw no future for her there. Adoption, he kept telling her, could be a way to use all the skills she'd learned.

"I'm sorry, but we don't do China adoption," Deborah Jost, the agency's Colorado child-placement supervisor, told Joshua. "But call me back if you want to start an agency; maybe I can help."

Joshua dialed more agencies, each time explaining that his wife was a lawyer from China who could help start a Chinese adoption program. One agency showed some interest, but Lily was disappointed when nothing came of it. After dropping the twins at preschool one morning, she mentioned her frustration to a mother who she knew had adopted a son. The woman's response gave Lily yet another avenue to pursue: Ask the Colorado licensing department to recommend an agency.

The following week Lily and Joshua sat in the state licensing office, explaining their idea to Margaret Bremmer. They were sure that if they could find a willing adoption agency, Lily would be a huge asset to help start up a China adoption program.

But Mrs. Bremmer knocked them off balance, taking a different tack: Why not do it yourselves?

Lily and Joshua glanced sideways at each other. It was the second time that someone had suggested that they could open their own agency.

"A Chinese attorney doing Chinese adoption makes all the sense in the world to me," Mrs. Bremmer told the couple. As Lily and Joshua sat stunned, their minds racing, she explained where to get the documentation they would need and then sent them on their way.

When they got into the car, Joshua turned to Lily.

"Maybe we should do it. Maybe we should start our own agency," he said, the idea taking hold in his mind. "I know we could do it."

But Lily hesitated. "I don't know," she said. "It would be so much work. And is it really the best way?"

Five months had passed since Joshua had come home with the *People's Daily* story on the new law. Lily was still trying to get her software company going, but she felt a stirring inside, a whisper of current softly pulling her forward.

At home that summer, she studied the requirements to become an adoption agency. For the first time, she and Joshua started jotting down possible names: Hope for Children, Second Chance, New Beginnings, Family Happiness, China's Child.

It was Chinese Children Adoption International that they presented to Dr. Covell on a blazing hot August afternoon in the library of Denver Seminary.

"It's a good name," Dr. Covell said, his eyes encouraging. "People will know exactly what you do."

It was the confirmation they needed, and Joshua's marketing mind sprung into action. Now, they needed a motto. They started out with the word love. Lily came up with the rest: *Love brings all of us together.*

Their mission was simple: Be the bridge of love that brings orphaned Chinese children and American parents together.

When they began working on a brand, Lily's father recognized that his daughter and son-in-law really were serious. Given his run-ins with the communist government, the whole idea seemed like trouble. An adoption agency doing business with China could put Lily — and the rest of his family — at risk.

"Don't worry. I'll take the lead and put my name out front," Joshua said, wanting to protect his wife and ease his in-laws' worries. "If something goes wrong in China, I'll be the one to take the blame."

Reluctantly, Guang Qian shifted gears, realizing he had help he could offer. He took out the fine brush, solid black ink and stone he used each day to practice his calligraphy. On a square sheet of white paper, he painted the Chinese character *ai* — love — that became the brand for CCAI.

Guang Qian had learned in the army that attention to detail could be the difference between life and death. Knowing the same was true in a business sense, he wrote out the principles that the agency would live by:

Always have more than one plan.

Make sure you calculate your time so you have enough to achieve every goal.

Finish your work ahead of your deadline in case something goes wrong.

Double and triple check that you're doing the right thing before you do it.

Walk the extra mile.

The sky was brilliant blue without a wisp of a cloud on the autumn day that Margaret Bremmer arrived at the Zhong home for an inspection. The young Chinese man was clearly nervous, and his words tumbled out so quickly she could hardly understand him. He had no idea what this woman from the state would think of the unfinished basement office he and Lily had cobbled together.

In a borrowed truck, Joshua and Lily hauled in a secondhand desk from Riverside Baptist Church that seemed heavy as a coffin. On it, they set up a computer from Lily's software company, a fax machine that would double as a copier, and a phone with one line and the number 347-CCAI. At a garage sale, they had picked up a used four-drawer file cabinet — including two hundred folders — for four dollars.

On September 15, 1992, Lily and Joshua had filed incorporation papers for Chinese Children Adoption International. Listed as the first board members were Dr. Covell, chairman of the board; Joshua, president; and Lily, executive director. Serving as honorary board member was Nie Guang Qian. There was no money to hire an attorney to complete the application for an adoption license, so Lily and Joshua did it themselves.

Trusting that they had done all that they could do, Lily felt a sense of peace. But she could see the tension growing in her husband's face as he watched Mrs. Bremmer. The woman from the state scanned the entire room without speaking. Lily knew what Joshua was thinking.

Would it be enough? What more can we do?

Minutes passed before Mrs. Bremmer finally turned to the young couple.

"You can operate fine here," she told them. CCAI's adoption license application had won approval.

For the state of Colorado, it was the successful completion of another inspection. But for Lily and Joshua, it was a gigantic leap of faith. They were diving in headfirst, with no sense of what they'd discover beneath the surface.

The huge, second-hand fax machine in the basement grunted, then screeched out a long beep. CCAI's first fax from China had arrived. It came from Hunan's capital city, Changsha, one of one hundred forty cities that Lily's father had identified as having a population over one million. Joshua had sent letters to them all, respectfully requesting permission to visit their orphanages. Hunan was the first to respond, and it seemed like a good sign. The south-central province was the place where Lily's father had grown up and the birthplace of Chairman Mao.

The local Ministry of Civil Affairs wrote that it would be honored to escort Mr. Zhong to its orphanages. At last, it seemed, CCAI was in business.

Joshua had made his travel plans when he received a notice from China that stopped him cold. The Ministry of Civil Affairs in Beijing had banned all provinces from any communication with Chinese Children Adoption International. The central government officials had learned about the letters Joshua sent directly to local officials, and the message was clear: No one was allowed to bypass Beijing. An investigation was underway in the nation's capital to determine whether the Colorado adoption agency was legitimate. Meanwhile, no one was to speak to CCAI.

"Before we even go, they stop us," Joshua groaned.

"If it is God's will, the door will be opened for us," Lily said calmly. "If God closes the door, there's nothing we can do."

Joshua was not as trusting. Dreading what he would hear, he called the Hunan Civil Affairs office to check on his visit. The invitation, he was told, was still open. There was no mention of the ban by Beijing. Reassured by their response, Joshua renewed his plans to return to his homeland.

A blizzard raged on the November day that Lily drove Joshua to the Denver airport for his flight to Los Angeles, connecting to China. As Joshua studied the departing flights monitor, the flashing message ignited him.

"Delayed?" Joshua shouted. "No way I'm missing my connection," he said as he quickly scanned the terminal.

"How will you get there?" Lily asked, her voice steady as she tried to counter Joshua's emotions.

"Drive!"

Joshua jerked up his suitcase and darted off, searching for the sign to direct him to car rentals. If he left right away, he could drive the sixteen hours to California in time for his flight to China. He strode off to the rental desk. As she followed him, Lily found another monitor and checked once more. With a sigh of relief, she saw that once again the flight to L.A. was back on schedule. She hurried after Joshua, catching him before he could implement his desperate plan.

The government vehicle pulled slowly to a stop in front of a one-story brick house in the poorest part of Changsha. Joshua climbed out of the car into the steady rain and silently followed his two escorts from the Hunan Department of Civil Affairs into the squalid building.

In an instant, the stench of human waste made his stomach clench. He gritted his teeth and stepped forward. Underneath his winter coat, he shivered in the damp, cold air. There was no heat in this place, not even a coal stove or coal pot in sight. He followed the pair into a room no bigger than three hundred square feet. Built in a U shape along three grimy walls was a wooden shelf painted green.

It took a few moments before Joshua's mind could wrap itself around what he was seeing. There, laying side by side on the narrow bench were more than thirty babies. A single, dim bulb dangling from the low ceiling cast an eerie yellow pall over them. Thick blankets covered nearly every inch of the tiny beings; all that was visible were pair after pair of small, dark, waiting eyes. Some of the infants cried out, but no nanny was in sight to answer their calls. A few struggled to move their arms and legs under the heavy weight of the blankets, but most were motionless.

Joshua's heart was pounding and his mind racing as he was ushered into four more rooms just like the first. So many children. Everywhere he looked there were small, forgotten lives, bundled up against the harshness of their world. Even though these children were the survivors, most of the babies lay still, as if they had already given up.

Inside two other cold brick houses, dozens more babies were lined up like old books stored on a shelf. In all there were close to two hundred infants, nearly all of them girls. Joshua couldn't help but think of his own children back at home, warm and dry in their comfortable beds. A wave of sickness in his gut, reality crashed in. Some of the babies warehoused in these barren rooms would not live. As he left them behind, his guides confirmed that terrible truth: One-third of the babies would die before they reached six months.

That night Joshua called Lily and struggled to convey the grimness of what he had witnessed.

He nearly choked on the words.

"It was a human hell," he told her. "A few were screaming, but no one picked them up. Some looked sick, but there was no medicine. Many were thin and listless. They seemed to be starving."

When Joshua hung up, he felt relieved to have had Lily to talk with. The stillness of her demeanor helped him refocus. But he feared what tomorrow's schedule would bring.

The next day, the officials escorted their American visitor to another orphanage in the city of Xiangtan. Inside the small house, Joshua found the same wooden shelves piled with babies. In the middle of one room, toddlers no bigger than Art and Amy sat on bamboo potty chairs, their heads wilting down on their chests. Cloth strips bound their tiny wrists and their ankles to the chairs. Their noses were runny, their eyes without expression. The pots they sat above reeked of waste.

"Why are they tied?" he asked. "How long have they been here?"

"Since breakfast."

It was now late morning. Joshua could only stare and try to keep a respectful stance. The cloth strips seemed to be the only thing holding the slumped children in the chairs.

Their next stop was the Zhuzhou orphanage. The single small building was stark but a bit cleaner than the filthy houses he had left behind. Walking into a room filled with cribs, he felt his hopes rise. But as he approached a crib and peered over the edge, he realized that each crib was home to two or three babies. As the group passed from room to room, Joshua saw that there were no toys on the floor or color on the soiled walls. But still he was relieved to see that the alert babies seemed to be better off.

The Civil Affairs officials drove on bumpy back roads most of the following day until they reached the rural town of Yueyang. They stayed overnight in a government hotel with holes in the ground for toilets and no hot water. In the morning, Joshua walked into another orphanage with no cribs. A caretaker moved alongside the long shelf of babies, propping a bottle of steaming-hot formula into the mouth of each child. Fifteen minutes later, the worker made a second round, retrieving the bottles. Some were only half empty, but it did not matter. At fifteen minutes, the meal was over — even if the bottle had rolled away from an infant's mouth. Nowhere did Joshua see even a single infant being fed in someone's arms.

On the long drive back to Changsha, Joshua was silent, allowing the officials to chatter away as if he wasn't there. As the countryside flowed past, he could not shake from his mind the image of the babies on the wooden shelves. He would not leave China without getting what he had come for.

When he told Lily what he had seen, he realized only part of what he had been feeling. During his tours it was as if he were drowning as he wrestled with the emotions that washed over him. Now, talking to Lily, he was overcome with shame. What he had witnessed in his homeland was wrong.

"We're Chinese, and we can't even take care of our own children. We've got to get them out of here, Lily."

"We'll try," Lily promised. "We'll do all we can."

By the time he headed to the airport, Joshua's suitcase carried a contract to adopt forty children from Hunan orphanages.

Hang on. We'll be back.

Back home in Denver, Joshua showed Lily the snapshots he had taken in the orphanages. Only when she held those images in her hands and looked through that window across the world did Lily understand what Joshua had meant by human hell. Peering into those faces, she felt the desperation the babies were powerless to express. But when she flipped to the photo of the toddlers bound to their potty chairs, her hands trembled at the injustice. Inside her came a sudden swell of urgency. The pictures were a confirmation that was undeniable. Lily knew God was calling to them. They must do all that they could to rescue their *tong xiang* — their countrymen needed them.

You have a beautiful baby girl.

SEVEN

FIGHTING DRAGONS
1993

Eileen Berling sat in the morning worship service at Cherry Hills Community Church with her husband Chuck, reading the Sunday bulletin. She scanned the listings that she'd seen so many times, but this time one in particular caught her eye:

If you are between 35 and 50 years old and have room in your heart and home for an abandoned Chinese girl, please call 347-CCAI.

Joshua had wondered if anyone would even care that January day they posted the first CCAI ad in their church bulletin. He did not understand at all why Americans adopted. The infertility rate among U.S. couples was high, and he knew that divorce — uncommon in China — was accepted in America. But was it childless couples or couples in second marriages who adopted? Or were Americans simply generous, loving people like the Laymans, willing to be a family to a child they had not birthed?

"What if they take them and change their mind?" Joshua asked one night as he lay awake in bed. "What if they want to give them back?"

"They won't," Lily said, pausing. "Will they?"

"We'd better be prepared to accept them in our home," Joshua said, his voice dead serious.

Joshua listened to the voice message from Eileen Berling on CCAI's answering machine. It was five thirty on the evening of January 18, 1993. The friendly woman said she'd seen the ad in the Sunday bulletin. He jotted down the number she left then dialed it.

"Is this a good time to talk?" Joshua asked.

"Sure. I'm just cooking dinner."

"Well, I hope it's Chinese," Joshua quipped.

Eileen laughed. She explained that she and her husband were each in their second marriage. Both had grown children from previous marriages, and Chuck would soon turn fifty.

"I told Chuck, 'If we hurry we can make the cut!'" she said, chuckling again.

The couple hadn't been looking to adopt, but they talked about the ad as they drove home from church. For some reason, the idea resonated with them. Chuck surprised Eileen when he said, "Let's call from the car."

The Berlings became CCAI's first official family. By February, they were sitting in an orientation meeting at Denver Seminary with a half dozen other hopeful couples.

"There are a lot of things you can be to an adoptive child, but you can never be her birth mother," said Deborah Jost, the Bethany Christian Services supervisor who had become CCAI's child-placement adviser. "An adoptive child has a hole in her heart."

Eileen cringed. She knew how much that hole could hurt. Her grandparents had raised her after her own mother had a mental breakdown. After her grandparents died, the alcoholic woman who owned their family's house took in the orphaned girl. It was a painful story Eileen would recount in the biography adoptive parents were required to write. Chuck also had tasted a similar pain, having grown up with an alcoholic father.

But the Berlings put their hurts behind them to raise their own families and pursue successful careers. Now they were in their late forties, too old for a baby in the minds of their family and friends. But by March, they and five other couples in CCAI's Group One had finished their home studies.

With a mix of excitement and nerves, Lily called the Hunan Ministry of Civil Affairs.

"We're ready to send our families' information," she told them.

"Can they come next week?" the official asked, unaware that the request was anything but ordinary.

"Next week? How can we do that?" Lily asked, taken aback.

"After that, you can't come," he said flatly.

"What do you mean?"

There was no way she could have seen what was coming.

"After next week, we're shutting down."

China was on the brink of a total adoption overhaul. The process was being centralized, and the government needed time to standardize the procedures. Until the new rules were published, no adopted babies could leave China.

As Lily hung up, her mind raced, searching for a solution. Any solution. She dialed the Chinese Embassy in Washington, D.C.

"How long will China be closed?" she asked them.

"We don't know. Six months … maybe a couple of years."

What in the world are we going to do? What do we tell the families?

She struggled to quell the fears that gripped her as she sifted through their options. They would have to find some way to refund the fees the families had paid. There was nothing to do but close the files and transfer the home studies to another agency. The families could adopt a child from a different country, and CCAI would shut down.

All the while, Joshua tried to convince her not to quit.

"We have to keep going," he kept saying.

But Lily was adamant. They could not leave these six families hanging indefinitely.

As they agonized, Lily said a silent prayer.

I didn't think we should do this in the first place. But we've come so far. God, it's your will. Show us what to do.

She dreaded doing it, but Lily knew she had to call the families. She couldn't keep them in the dark.

Slowly, she dialed the Berlings. When Eileen answered, Lily recounted her conversations with the Chinese officials. Then she paused, not knowing what to expect. Eileen quickly broke the silence.

"We'll wait," Eileen said matter-of-factly. "We want a Chinese baby."

"But we don't know how long this could take," Lily said, wanting to be sure she had been clear.

"We'll wait," she said cheerfully. "No worries."

Unable to believe what she'd just heard, Lily dialed another family. To her surprise, the answer was the same.

"Korea closed for six months and reopened," the woman told Lily. "That's just the way it is with international adoption. Trust me."

Trust me. It wasn't that she didn't trust the families. It was the Chinese bureaucracy Lily could not trust. She'd dealt with China's government as an attorney, and she knew first-hand that state matters could drag on for years. But she looked to the families as the response to her prayer. If the families in Group One wanted to wait, she had no choice but to stay open. After all, she reasoned, if there is no Group One, there is no CCAI.

In the meantime, Lily shifted her attention to finishing school, and in early June she finally earned her MBA. Still, there was no word from China. The hot, dry summer dragged by, and she tried to keep her mind disciplined, refusing to let it wonder whether CCAI would ever see its first adoption.

As Colorado's aspens turned flaming gold then shed their leaves, CCAI's chances for survival seemed to be fluttering away. Lily came to accept the long wait for news from China, just as she'd learned to endure the seemingly endless gray winters of her childhood.

The temperatures were below freezing in Fushun one November morning as Lily's father sat, as he had for so many days now, scanning the newspaper for the news he wanted so badly. Finally, on this day, he found what he was looking for.

Implementation Measures for Foreigners to Adopt in China

At last, he had news that would help his daughter. Excitedly, he ripped the story from the paper and faxed it to his daughter in Denver.

The first call Lily made was to Eileen Berling.

"I knew it!" Eileen exclaimed. "I knew they'd reopen!"

Nearly a year had gone by since the Berlings had first seen the ad in the church bulletin. For most of 1993, the phone at Chinese Children Adoption International had not rung at all. Now it seemed the agency, and the members of Group One, had been given new life.

But the ecstatic families had no idea of the huge obstacles that still towered before them. Only Lily and Joshua knew of the problems that CCAI had had with the Civil Affairs Ministry in Beijing. Joshua knew that his run-in with the central government could do more than just chill the agency's relationship with China. It could destroy it. On top of that, the families had no idea that China's new rules required that adoptive families be approved not only by Civil Affairs but also by the Ministry of Justice. And at that moment, the Ministry of Justice didn't know the adoptive families in CCAI's Group One even existed.

Lily and Joshua were in desperate need of help.

"It's OK," Lily told Joshua one day after a phone call with her parents. "God has sent us Mr. Gu."

Gu Jian Ping was the son of Luo Rui Fen, Lily's mother's best friend. Rui Fen and Liang Zhen had helped each other survive as they sang and danced for the communist soldiers in the Korean War. Now, it was Liang Zhen's daughter who needed their help.

Rui Fen, who lived with her family in Beijing, asked her son what he could do to help Lily and Joshua. He was able to make a connection with an official at the Ministry of Justice who arranged a meeting between CCAI and the head of China's adoption office. It seemed that Mr. Gu was able to help them clear the first hurdle.

But Joshua knew there was no way he could show his face in Beijing. The CCAI letter he sent to local governments had so offended the central government that Joshua told Mr. Gu to tell officials that he'd resigned as agency president as a gesture of contrition.

The Chinese government did not trust its own people, but Joshua had an idea. He thought the Ministry of Justice just might trust a respected American professor who spoke fluent Mandarin. Once again, he turned to Dr. Covell for help.

"We have no money for an airline ticket for you," Joshua said, embarrassed as he explained their conundrum and his plan.

"I see only one problem," Dr. Covell said, his voice grave.

Joshua waited, his mind whirring, fearing the worst.

"I have to find a substitute to teach my class," he said smiling.

On March 16, 1994, a few days before Joshua and Dr. Covell left for China, CCAI received a six-page fax from the Ministry of Civil Affairs. But unlike so many other recent correspondences, these pages didn't bring consternation or worry. On each page, among the Chinese characters, was a black-and-white photograph the size of a postage stamp. And in each photograph, a small face.

Eileen Berling was the first to get what would come to be known as "The Call."

"You have a beautiful baby girl," Lily told her.

Later that day, Eileen saw her daughter's face for the first time. She squinted at the blurry picture. All she could make out under the hat on the baby's head was a nose and a chin. She called her husband.

"So what does she look like?" he asked anxiously.

"A thumb with a hat on it," Eileen replied.

The orphanage called her Puyang, the Chinese word for universal spirit. It was after a Sunday morning service on Zoë, Greek for spiritual life, that the Berlings chose the name for their new daughter. Now that the couple finally had a face to attach to their dreams, Eileen found her mind racing off into the unknown. She wondered if Zoë's biological mother had given her baby a name. She wondered if the mother had even held the child before she and the baby were separated.

The families in Group One were scheduled to pick up their children in Hunan in just a few weeks. But they still did not know that CCAI was not welcome by the Justice Ministry.

At the Beijing airport, Joshua and Dr. Covell loaded their suitcases into a battered yellow minivan and climbed into seats that were made simply of metal bars. Not much later, the driver pulled up to the Hui Jia Lou Hotel, a rundown, two-story building in the shadow of the first five-star high-rise hotel in the nation's capital. When the front-desk clerk gave each of the exhausted men a key to the same room, Dr. Covell looked surprised. Realizing the dean of the seminary had expected his own room, Joshua started to apologize.

"I was a missionary," Dr. Covell reminded him. "I've slept on the floor many nights in China. I'll be glad to have a bed."

The next morning, Gu Jian Ping arrived to escort Dr. Covell to the Justice Ministry. Joshua watched nervously as his American friend started toward one of the worn, yellow minivans. But Mr. Gu stepped forward and stopped him. They must arrive at the Justice Ministry in a respectable taxi, he explained, to establish their status.

A block before they arrived at the ministry, Joshua asked the driver to stop and drop him off. He knew he didn't dare show his face for this meeting. The taxi delivered the two men to the Justice Ministry, where they were ushered into the international adoption office. There the director sat working at her desk. Mrs. Liu did not rise to greet them, an immediate sign of deep disrespect. When she looked up, her eyes were smoldering. In Mandarin, Dr. Covell carefully explained that Chinese Children Adoption International was in the process of getting started. He had flown from the United States to try to work out procedures that would be acceptable to the Justice Ministry.

"Then why," she shot back, "are you here at the very time that your first group of families is already coming?

"We, ah…"

"How did this happen?" she barked. "Why are you doing this without our approval?"

Dr. Covell was for a moment speechless. How could he defend what he knew to be true? Joshua and Lily had made their own adoption arrangements with Hunan officials with the approval of the Ministry of Civil Affairs, despite the ban on CCAI. The official knew it, and she was livid.

The dean of the Denver Seminary tried again. CCAI was a legitimate American agency, he explained, with a board of directors that oversaw the decision-making. He apologized that CCAI did not know it needed permission from both the Ministry of Civil Affairs and the Justice Ministry. The official's eyes bored through him.

121

She would not budge. Soon, Dr. Covell and Mr. Gu were dismissed, feeling as if they had simply been throwing themselves against the side of a mountain.

When they picked up Joshua to go back to the hotel, Dr. Covell's frustration was visible. He threw up his arms, exasperated. "This agency is never going to make it," he told Joshua.

Joshua felt like he was trapped under water. He had embarrassed his loyal friend and offended the powerful bureaucracy that controlled the lives of the orphans he'd come to rescue. He felt himself sink deeper as he realized it might not be humanly possible for CCAI to keep its promise to the Group One families.

There was nothing Joshua could do. The fate of CCAI and the babies rested on the shoulders of two distressed men whose arguments had failed to change the Justice official's mind.

That evening, Joshua called Lily to debrief her. Lily offered what encouragement she could from so far away, and silently she wrestled with the fear that after all their waiting, all their work, they might fall short of bringing these babies to their families. On her desk calendar on March 23, she wrote in Chinese:

Pray for the Justice Ministry and our families' dossiers.

The following morning, Dr. Covell and Mr. Gu decided to try to sway the official one last time. After all, how much worse could it get?

Heavy-hearted, they climbed into another expensive cab and headed back to the Ministry of Justice. There was a sense of dread as they paused again outside Mrs. Liu's door. When they appeared in her office again, the official was incensed. She could hardly believe they had the gall to keep pressing the case she had already declared closed.

But Mr. Gu pressed ahead, refusing to be deterred by the woman's anger. He knew he must try. In a low voice of respect, he spoke on, explaining they understood that CCAI unintentionally had been disrespectful of the Justice Ministry and that the agency needed to work through these problems. Again and again he apologized, always respectfully, emphasizing that they were willing to do whatever was necessary to resolve the impasse.

Standing back, Dr. Covell felt a slight sense of relief to have Mr. Gu, rather than himself, in the line of fire. It also gave him a chance to study what was happening inside the office that seemed to hold the key to CCAI's future. Dr. Covell watched the official carefully. As she listened to Mr. Gu and his repeated apologies, it seemed her stiff, military bearing softened — almost imperceptibly. But it was not his imagination. Mr. Gu saw it too. Encouraged, he continued with his placating words, still expecting that at any moment the woman would stop him and throw them out.

Finally, about the time Mr. Gu realized he did not know what more he could possibly say, Mrs. Liu stood and silenced him.

Her voice was reluctant. "You've come this far. … There's no sense in trying to stop you now. But you must learn from this mistake."

Stunned, the men stood and bowed. Then her words truly sank in.

"*Xie xie,*" they said in unison, their hearts leaping. "Thank you!"

Moments after they arrived back at their hotel, Joshua was on the phone to Lily. He didn't care what time it was in the U.S. On her calendar, Lily scribbled a note in English on March 24:

God is answering our prayer.

On their last morning in Beijing, Dr. Covell wanted to celebrate. He treated his elated Chinese companions to a five-star breakfast in the gleaming high-rise hotel next door. As he sat down with a full plate, Joshua was convinced that never in his life had noodles tasted so heavenly.

Joshua and Dr. Covell soon were boarding a plane headed to Kunming, Denver's sister city and CCAI's next adoption target. As Joshua settled in next to his friend who served on the sister-city committee, he became unusually quiet. This critical skirmish had been won, but it was just the beginning. When he thought about the task looming before him, it was enough for him to forget their hard-earned strides. Soon he would be in Changsha with six families in tow — families who knew nothing about China's culture, its customs, or its language. They would be relying entirely on him and his ability to clear any roadblocks that could upset the precarious balance of the fragile agreement they had just struck.

I do my part.
The rest is up to God.

EIGHT

STANDS UP STRAIGHT
1994

On March 27, CCAI's first families stepped into the polluted streets of Changsha. They had done their best to prepare for the unknown, and in their swollen suitcases was the proof — each was packed with one hundred disposable diapers, a carton of baby wipes, six plastic bottles, a dozen nipples, two cans of infant formula, baby shampoo, lotion, clothes, blankets, and toys. For everything else, they put their trust in CCAI.

Joshua guided them to their three-star hotel, the Xiang Pan, where he scurried from room to room helping the families in Group One get settled. After assuring himself they could fend for themselves for a few minutes, he headed off to a hotel conference room to meet with local officials. He had no problem getting the families registered for their adoptions. But when the notary arrived, Joshua was greeted with words that froze his heart.

"They're not qualified," the local notary, Mr. Zhang, told him.

"What do you mean?"

"Your families don't meet the requirements under the new rules. They cannot adopt the babies."

Joshua felt as if he'd been struck by a bolt of lightning. Less than two weeks earlier, the Justice Ministry officials had agreed to let the CCAI families come. But now the local officials said the Justice Ministry had ordered them not to notarize the adoptions. Under the new rules, they reminded Joshua, adoptive parents must be childless, over thirty-five and under fifty. Some of these families had children; some were too young.

In a panic, Joshua raced to his room, hoping that none of the families would see him in the hall. Once safely in his room, he called Colorado.

"What is it?" Lily asked, immediately hearing the strain in his voice. "What's wrong?"

"They won't let us adopt our babies because of the new rules," Joshua said. "We have to figure something out — fast."

As he explained the government's argument, his words ignited the lawyer inside Lily. Her mind seized the challenge the Justice Ministry had thrown before them.

Let them say there's no case, and I will make one. I will find a way to argue. I will find a way to fight. I will not give in.

In the chaos that followed, Lily remained a reservoir of calm. For nearly two days, she lived in CCAI's basement office. By day, she worked at her desk, strategizing and making notes.

Late into the night, long after the children were asleep, Lily was still answering rings for help from overseas. Bent over her desk into the early morning hours, she wrote out her arguments in Chinese. She knew the legal system, and she held a notary certificate. She would use all that she'd learned as an attorney in China to free the babies from the bureaucratic trap that ensnared them.

She pulled out a stack of clean paper. On the top of each sheet, she wrote the name of a family. From the file cabinet, she pulled out the thick family dossiers she'd compiled for Joshua to translate into Mandarin. She studied them, then she listed every reason she could think of to prove each family was qualified.

The last thing she did before she fell into bed for a few precious hours of sleep was fax pages and pages of notes to Joshua and Mr. Gu, who had come to Changsha to help CCAI. The next morning at the hotel, they picked up the faxes to prepare for their fight.

Lily continued to dig in, rooted in her refusal to let anything stand in the way of bringing home CCAI's first babies. She refused to even fleetingly think of failing the American families who had put their trust in CCAI. She coached Joshua on how to deliver her arguments to the Chinese officials and how to explain the latest setbacks to CCAI's families.

He gathered the families in one hotel room to share the news.

"There's been a miscommunication between two ministries," he told them, speaking carefully. "Your adoptions are being delayed. We appreciate your patience while we work things out."

The words were intended to calm them, but Joshua's feelings ran too close to the surface. He had never been able to mask his emotions, and the strain on his face told them something was very wrong. The families pressed him relentlessly until finally he could no longer keep the truth from them.

"The notary is refusing to allow you to adopt your babies," he told the shaken families. "They claim you don't qualify under the new rules."

According to China, the Berlings broke the rules. Between the two of them, they had three children from their first marriages. The couple could get a special-needs child, but they did not qualify to take home the healthy child they'd been promised.

Eileen could not speak. Her eyes welled up as she stared at the blurry face in the match picture she had carried with her for weeks.

I might never see the real you.

The sickening realization that the families might not get their babies rippled through the room. The sound of soft cries washed over the families, dragging Joshua's emotions into a spiral.

Distraught, Eileen turned to her husband. "It's like you're in the delivery room, and the doctor says, 'The hospital is closing. You cannot have your baby.'"

The families gathered every thirty minutes for an update. Joshua rushed back and forth between the notaries in the negotiating room and one of the families' rooms, where all of Group One would cram in.

In Colorado, Lily wrote out new arguments for Joshua and Mr. Gu. For the Berlings, she wrote:

129

They are in a second marriage. There are no children from this marriage. In their current marriage, they are childless. That makes them qualified to adopt.

For hours the negotiations dragged on. Most of the day in China — most of the night in Denver — Joshua and Lily talked on the phone. Each time she hung up, she prayed.

⌒

It was nearly three in the morning when Lily fell into bed. Her body was exhausted, but she could not sleep. Her mind kept swirling through all that was happening in China. In Beijing, the Justice official blocking CCAI's way had demanded that Civil Affairs send Group One's dossiers to her office. In Changsha, the families were clinging to the thumbnail-sized pictures of their babies, despairing over whether they would ever hold their daughters.

For a year and a half, they had waited. Lily felt the responsibility like a wall of water crushing in around her. Her mind flew to the worst case. "If they don't get their babies," she thought, "we'll return their money, even if we have to borrow it." But even that option did not ease the burden.

Once again, she shifted gears, turning the puzzle over and over in her mind. Slowly, steadily she pressed on, looking for the crack in their argument.

I must find a way to convince the Justice Ministry to let our babies go. What else can I do?

She came up with still more arguments. By now, the head of the adoption office in the Justice Ministry knew Lily Nie by name. It was clear that everything Mr. Gu told Mrs. Liu in his urgent phone calls to Beijing was being fed to him by the Chinese attorney in America.

"The American families are here," Mr. Gu told the Justice official. "Civil Affairs has matched them with children. They started the process before China centralized adoption. Please, please reconsider honoring these matches."

"I did not invite them here," she said flatly.

"But Civil Affairs did," Mr. Gu parried. "We understand that Justice and Civil Affairs are having a disagreement, but you have six foreign families here. You and Civil Affairs must come to an agreement and present one decision from the People's Republic of China."

Mrs. Liu was unmoved.

Finally, Mr. Gu launched Lily's final argument. He took a deep breath.

"If you tell these American families you will not finalize their adoption and they cannot go home with their children, are you willing to shoulder the international consequences?"

Mr. Gu waited restlessly for a response and desperately tried to read the official's voice, hoping that the notion of losing face might weaken her resolve. But it seemed useless. As he hung up the phone, he steeled himself for the next day, when they would try once again to make their case.

The following morning, Joshua and Mr. Gu again marched in to plead with the notaries in Changsha.

"These parents were told by Civil Affairs to come to China to get their children," Mr. Gu implored. "They applied before the law changed. Isn't there anything we can do?"

The stern officials looked at each other, hesitating. Finally one spoke.

"Let's go," he said.

"Where?" Joshua asked, confused.

Could there possibly be someone else we need to argue with?

"To the orphanage," he said.

Joshua and Mr. Gu glanced at each other. Joy erupted in an instant as they figured out what happened. The notaries had gotten the word from the Justice Ministry official. Mrs. Liu would no longer stand in the way of CCAI.

Joshua rushed into the room where the weary parents were keeping vigil. He wore a mint green sweater and a shiny gold chain hung from his neck. He flashed them the familiar grin — the one they had not seen for nearly two days, although it seemed more like an eternity. With his hair stylishly permed, for a fleeting moment it occurred to Eileen Berling that he looked like a rock star. The families fell silent.

"We're going to the orphanage!" he sang, triumphant.

The whoops went up, but Joshua quickly gestured for quiet.

"I can't make any promises," he said, suddenly turning cautious. "But let's go."

The van lurched along the bumpy back roads toward Xiangtan. As the hours passed, Eileen Berling's stomach grew queasy. It seemed to Eileen and her husband that the honking never stopped as their driver jockeyed around potholes and past buses, carts, bikes, and a handful of private cars. She strained to look out across the foreign landscape, wondering what the orphanage would look like.

At last, they slowed and pulled into a complex of buildings that surrounded a garden of green cabbages planted in neat rows. Joshua breathed a sigh of relief. This orphanage appeared to be nicer than any he had visited on his first trip. The families anxiously followed him to one of the buildings. At the door, the orphanage director stepped out to greet them, talking quickly with Joshua. It was the moment they had been waiting for. But instead of showing them to their babies, the director invited them to tea. Joshua tried to assure them, explaining it was the standard protocol when welcoming foreign visitors. The anticipation had made them edgy, but Eileen and Chuck and the others dutifully followed along.

In a conference room, the families sat around a table covered with a pink cloth, sipping tea and eating hard biscuits and orange slices. They smiled, tight-lipped, waiting. They listened to Joshua and the director, anxious for the time to pass. Finally, the director stood. In an instant all the couples were standing, fighting their desire to run alongside their host.

As they walked outside and passed into another building, the Berlings looked around, trying to memorize everything they saw — the buildings, the smells, the sounds. To one side, they saw a small girl watching them, clutching a doll. The girl's tiny legs were badly bowed. The doll in her arms was headless. She stared at Eileen, her eyes imploring. The girl's gaze stabbed deep into her, and she wondered what the silent child was thinking.

Where are you going? What are you doing? Will you take me?

Eileen's chest tightened. Their footsteps echoed as they left the girl behind.

They followed Joshua up the stairs to an outdoor landing where the families waited. One by one, the names of the anxious parents were called.

"Mr. and Mrs. Berling."

They stepped forward. A nanny placed a baby into Eileen's trembling arms, and for the first time, she held the daughter she'd nearly lost hope of ever seeing. Her new-parent instincts taking over, she gave the baby a quick assessment. She was relieved that her baby looked OK.

Eileen studied Zoë's face. The child didn't smile, and she didn't cry. As a nurse, Eileen saw a patient's eyes as the window to the heart. Looking hard into her daughter's deep chocolate eyes was like peering down a dark well. Eileen saw no emotion. She saw the eyes of a survivor. She knew this baby was meant to be theirs. Looking up at her husband, she saw his eyes brimming with tears. For the first time since their arrival in China, Chuck Berling was crying.

Once all the families' daughters had been placed in their arms, a nanny led them to the tiny room with six green cribs where their babies had lived. Eileen lowered Zoë into a crib and began peeling away the layers of tattered clothes that had bound her. First she pulled off a thick jacket, then a ragged sweater, two shirts, and two pairs of leggings. At last all that was left was a crude diaper, tied on with a string. As she looked closer, a shudder raced up her spine. The dirty string had been there so long it was embedded in the skin of her daughter's stomach. Eileen peeled the string from her baby's skin. Cringing, she tossed it aside, and replaced the soiled cloth with a disposable diaper from her backpack.

I'll take care of you, sweetie. Mama will take care of you.

The wide-eyed nannies chattered and squealed with approval as Eileen dressed her daughter in new clothes. Tentatively, Eileen held up the frayed orphanage clothes, pointing to her backpack for permission to take them home. A nanny smiled and nodded yes. Carefully, she tucked them away, grateful to have even a few ragged remnants from the earliest moments of her daughter's life.

Minutes later, the families were led out of the room. In their arms, they carried out the babies they had come for. They could hardly believe that all the waiting was over. Exhausted, they wanted only to return to their hotel, but the officials insisted that they go to dinner. In a nearby restaurant, the Americans gathered around a table for a five-course Chinese banquet.

Already the newly formed families were getting to know each other. One child could not sit upright by herself, although she was nine months old. Supported by her mother, the girl's tiny hands lunged for food that she stuffed into her hungry mouth. Her mother guided her gently under the sparkling smile and watchful gaze of American actress Brooke Shields, whose poster hung on the restaurant wall behind them.

By this time, the babies were sweating. They had lived the entire winter without heat, but now they were wrapped in blankets and held closely by their new parents in a hot, crowded restaurant. After dinner, on the ride to the hotel, the heat on the bus made their warm skin wet and clammy. The worn-out families could barely wait to get back to their home away from home.

Eileen carried her baby to their room and laid her on the bed. Chuck pushed two chairs together to fashion a crib while Eileen stripped the clothes from their daughter. At four months, Zoë weighed fourteen pounds. As Eileen cradled her daughter's tiny head in her hand, she could feel that the back of it was flat. She turned Zoë over. The back of her head was bald, the hair worn away while she lay round the clock on her back in a crib. Eileen put her daughter in new pajamas and with what already seemed to be the five-hundredth kiss, gently laid her into the makeshift crib, where she slept through the night.

On Easter Sunday, rain poured from China's steely skies. Eileen stayed inside the hotel with Zoë, while Chuck and several parents went with Joshua to a church service in Changsha. Back in Denver, Lily recorded just two words on her calendar:

Praise God!

Eileen shook her head in disbelief. It was hard to fathom that this baby with silky skin sleeping in the makeshift crib next to her bed was really theirs. Staring at Zoë, Eileen realized for the first time since the moment she first held her how devastated she would be if anything happened to this child.

Now that they finally had Zoë, Chuck felt protective of his tiny daughter. He didn't want to risk going anywhere. The air on the streets of Changsha was thick with black smoke from the charcoal pots of food vendors. Roasted pig heads dripping with fat hung above the counters in the meat market. It seemed that everywhere they turned, Chinese were smoking cigarettes. The rumbling buses blew sooty fumes into the already heavily polluted air, honking as they looped in and out to avoid bikers frantically ringing their bells. After all they'd been through, their hotel room seemed much safer.

Nearly a week had passed since their arrival in China, and the Berlings wanted nothing more than to be home. Leaving Changsha, Group One's last stop would be Guangzhou, across the China Sea from Hong Kong, to get the babies' visas from the American Consulate.

Relieved to be on the final leg of their journey, the Berlings climbed into an elevator in the luxurious White Swan Hotel. Several Chinese women surrounded Zoë, patting her cheeks as they chattered in Chinese. One gave the thumbs up and managed in English: "Lucky baby."

A Chinese gentleman immaculately dressed in a fine Western-cut suit and an elegant tie spoke to them in impeccable English with a British accent. "You must understand," he said, "in this country, it's as if your daughter has won the lottery. She's a celebrity. She's going to live in America, and she'll get an education."

Later, at the medical clinic, the families waited in line for their turn with the Chinese doctor, their children cradled close. Some of the babies cried out in protest, but the examination was over in minutes. The final task before the consulate appointment was a visit to a photography shop, where the babies' visa pictures were taken.

In Colorado, Lily was preparing for the American Consulate officials to give them a hard time. How could she explain why six American families currently unqualified to adopt got Chinese babies? She re-read the immigration law. She tried to guess what the officials might focus on. Eventually she faxed to the White Swan Hotel answers to every question she imagined the consulate officials might ask. She had done what she could. She went to bed, weary but restless.

At two thirty in the morning in Denver, the ringing phone shook Lily awake.

"Lily, we got the visas!" Joshua practically shouted.

Finishing the phone call, Lily settled into a peaceful sleep.

We did it.

On April 8, 1994, Lily stood at the Denver airport holding the hands of her four-year-old twins, overwhelmed by the scene unfolding before her. Out of the gate streamed the American families, holding in their arms six black-haired, dark-eyed Chinese daughters.

Joshua rushed to Lily and the twins, wrapping his arms around them. The relief of getting Group One home swirled with the weight of what they had accomplished, and tears slipped down his cheeks. They had saved six lives.

As Lily touched the babies' sweet faces, the miracle of their arrival rippled deep inside her. Her mind flitted over the myriad tangles they had overcome, and Lily realized she had learned her first lesson in adoption. She would call it the "Hands Off" policy: She would do all she could to bring babies home from China and then let go.

I do my part. The rest is up to God.

Just three months later, in July, Lily and the twins found themselves back at the Denver airport, this time to welcome home Joshua and the families of Group Two as they returned from Yunnan's capital city of Kunming. The waiting area was filled with friends and families clutching bundles of colorful balloons and bouquets of fresh flowers. Everyone was straining to see the new arrivals. As the families filed by, the proud new parents held up their daughters for Lily to see. With Joshua beside her, Lily stood in awe that CCAI had now brought home eleven babies. Those eleven lives, and the lives of their families, would be forever changed. In China these abandoned girls had been considered all but worthless. Now they were treasured. Nothing seemed impossible.

But soon after, that invincible joy was slipping away. When Joshua returned, Lily felt something unsettling between them, something lurking beneath the surface. She pressed Joshua; he insisted that all was fine. But Lily could not shake the sensation that something was splintering between them.

Distraught and feeling like her marriage might become a casualty of the battles they had fought to bring these children home, Lily began thinking about shutting down the agency. Joshua wanted to keep CCAI open but Lily was becoming more and more convinced it was time to close the doors. She hadn't planned for adoption to be a long-term career, and finding homes for eleven abandoned Chinese children now seemed like it might be enough.

But on the morning of August 2, 1994, something stopped her. The phone in their basement office started to ring. At first it was a trickle, then a relentless stream. The callers wanted to know more about Chinese Children Adoption International. As soon as the phone was back in its cradle, it would ring out again. Lily had no idea what was going on until several callers mentioned the beautiful Chinese baby in the *Denver Post*.

While Lily fielded calls, Joshua jumped into the car and drove to the nearest gas station. He bought all the newspapers left in the *Denver Post* rack. On the cover of the features section was an article headlined "China Dolls." It told the story of the arrival of Chinese baby girls brought to Colorado by Chinese Children Adoption International.

By week's end, one-hundred hopeful, new families had submitted applications to bring Chinese babies into their families. Lily knew there was no way they could shut the doors now.

A few stressful months later, Joshua was back in Kunming, leading Group Three to their daughters. Everything was going smoothly, and Lily had started to feel like they were getting a good handle on the adoption process.

But while Joshua was in China, Lily discovered a love letter to her husband from a woman in Kunming. The unsettled feeling that had been lurking between Lily and Joshua now roared to the surface. The letter left no doubt in Lily's mind and heart that her husband had betrayed her trust while half a world away, and she did not hesitate.

She called Joshua in China and drilled him about the letter. Knocked off balance by Lily's unrelenting interrogation, Joshua revealed more about his time in Kunming. There, aiding the CCAI families, had been a young Chinese woman who had showered Joshua with affection. The realization that her husband had not refused the woman's attention left Lily dizzy — with anger, fear, and loneliness. She felt as if her seven-year marriage was washing away beneath her.

When Joshua returned to Colorado, Lily continued her drive to find out what had happened in Kunming. His insistence that the woman in Kunming meant nothing to him awakened a part of Lily that Joshua had never experienced. Her still, quiet strength erupted into fury, all crashing in on him. He begged for forgiveness, but Lily was resolute. Joshua swore that he loved her as he always had. But Lily was immovable.

As she lay in bed that night, she felt crushed and utterly alone. Divorce was unthinkable for a wife who had grown up in tradition-bound China. But she was ready for their marriage to end. In her heart, she felt it had.

Reeling, she wondered what to do next. In the anger and confusion of the days that followed, Lily found herself leaning ever more on her faith, praying for help and strength. In that time, she had one absolute moment of clarity. Regardless of the pain in her personal life, she knew she could not let down the hundred families now depending on CCAI — and she could not trust her husband in China.

There is no other choice but to go to China myself. I am the right one, the only one. I have faith that God will help me do it.

The fact that she was a woman about to do in China what was considered a man's job did not daunt her. For centuries, Chinese girls had been considered of little or no value. But her parents had rooted in Lily the belief that a boy is no better than a girl.

Her mind was set in stone. She would go it alone. But what made her heart sink further was the thought of leaving behind what she loved most — her own children.

I too am a girl from China.
I cannot let them grow up feeling they are nothing.

NINE

FINDING HOME
1995

Lily knelt down and gathered her young son and daughter into her arms. It was January 15, and the twins were five years old. She pressed them close to her chest. Amy laid her head of long black hair on her mother's shoulder. Art rested his small chin on the other shoulder. For a few seconds, Lily closed her eyes, shutting out the hustle of the Denver airport to breathe them in.

"Listen to *Lao Lao*," she said, nodding toward their grandmother. "I'll call you every day."

She looked into the eyes of her parents, who had agreed to leave their home in Fushun to come to America to help care for their youngest daughter's children while she was in China.

"Promise you'll play the piano for me when I call?" she said, letting her children go. Every day since they were four, she had listened to her children practice their lessons.

Now she gazed down at them one last time. They seemed so small. Before they could see her cry, Lily turned away.

Her eyes determined, she managed a tight-lipped smile to Joshua as she filed through the gate with the first group of families she would lead to China. On Joshua's face was the friendly grin that had become a great comfort to the adoptive families. None of them suspected that the couple's marriage was in turmoil.

Seeing the anxiety on the faces of the Americans, Lily inhaled deeply and summoned her strength. Inside she was nervous, but she was not afraid. She vowed that she would not let them see any signs of doubt or weakness.

It is up to me now to get these families the babies we've promised them.

As the attendant took her ticket, Lily could not escape the painful coincidence. Her first CCAI trip was to Kunming, the very place where her marriage began to unravel. It would take all of her strength to set aside her bitterness and do what she must do.

Lily strode up the steps of the Kunming orphanage with twenty Americans following close behind. The modern building was clean and well-kept, just like the pictures Joshua had shown her. Three times now he had succeeded in bringing Chinese babies home to America. An inkling of doubt edged its way into her mind. Straightening her shoulders, she walked through the door.

If Joshua can do this, so can I.

From her husband, she knew exactly what to expect. She understood how to help the families complete the complicated paperwork. She knew about the open area on the second floor where the families would wait. And she had Mr. Gu, who had flown in from Beijing to meet Lily and help make things go smoothly. What she did not expect was the chaos that ensued when it came time to get the babies so they could be presented to their parents.

As the families waited outside, Mr. Gu called out the names of the children on the list and the head nurse scurried away to find the babies. Trailing behind her were Lily, Mr. Gu, and the orphanage director, climbing up and down the stairs and hurrying in and out of rooms to track down the children. In the confusion, Lily would ask the caretakers the name of each baby and compare the child to the picture in the paperwork to verify she was the right one.

Hurrying to keep up, she prayed silently.

Please, let nothing go wrong. Please …

All the while, the families stayed in the open area where Lily had told them to wait. The minutes ticked by slowly. For them, it was a sensation like free-falling, waiting for a parachute to open. Still no one returned. The families strained to hear footsteps, or even a baby's cry. They glanced uncomfortably at each other.

Footstep by footstep, one by one, the caretakers at last arrived, each carrying a baby bundled in a blanket. Finally. The families' faces turned luminous as the Americans held their daughters for the first time.

It seemed an eternity to Janet and David Schroeder before they heard their name called out. The childless couple in their thirties from Evergreen, Colorado, had never heard of the abandoned orphans in China until they read a story about Lily in a 1993 newsletter published by International Students Inc., the organization where Joshua worked.

Now, after a long wait during China's adoption shutdown, they were at last about to become parents. In Janet's arms, a caretaker placed a small bundle wrapped in a pink blanket. From inside gazed the face of their new daughter. Emily's large, dark eyes were serious but alert, taking in everything around her. At ten months, she was thirteen pounds, about the size of a six-month-old, but the soft cheeks below her knit hat were rosy. The quiet child was tiny, but she looked healthy.

Wandering from couple to couple, a nanny stopped to peek under the blankets to inspect each baby. When she came to Emily, she sung out happily, *"Qiu Ping! Qiu Ping!"* The woman hovered over the baby, giving her a squeeze.

"God is good," Janet said softly, grateful to know that her daughter was special to this woman.

Breathing a sigh of relief after all eleven babies had been delivered, Lily stepped closer, examining the children. In some faces, the dark almond eyes were flat, unlike the alert, darting eyes of her own children as babies. A pang of loneliness for Art and Amy welled up inside her, followed by a sudden stirring of something deeper. Touching their warm skin and looking into their eyes, Lily felt an unexpected connection to these once-forsaken girls.

I too am a girl from China. I cannot let them grow up feeling they are nothing. I must do my part to make them feel worthy.

The plane rose above the Kunming soil, and the rigid muscles in Lily's shoulders began to loosen. Her first group of adoptive parents and babies were safely on their way, and before long she would be holding her own children again. But shadowing that promise were conversations she'd had about the details of her husband's previous stay in Kunming. The local representative who met Lily for the first time was unable to make sense of it.

"You're so beautiful, so perfect," he said. "Why?"

Now, staring across the aisle at the almond-eyed baby resting in her new mother's arms, Lily knew it would be the same question that one day would haunt these abandoned daughters of China.

In Denver's airport, Lily pressed forward with the crowd of families. The moment they saw her, Art and Amy rushed to their mother. Lily held them tight and kissed them, drinking them in amid the joyous reunions at the airport gate and straining to hang on to the happiness around her.

That night, she asked Joshua to move out. He was crushed, and his desperate pleas for forgiveness went unheard. The time she'd spent in China had helped her decide that it was the right thing for her to do. Unable to dissuade her, Joshua left in despair.

The one thing the separated couple agreed on was the future of CCAI. The agency would remain open, although none of the families would know the founding couple were separated. They chose to keep their family's heartache to themselves while they worked to build families for others.

Swept into the world of China adoptions, Lily shut down her computer company and moved CCAI out of the basement into a nearby office building. She hired an assistant to help run the agency when she was away, while Joshua worked at International Students and translated dossiers for CCAI. A far more difficult decision for Lily was to place Art and Amy in daycare full time. She wanted to be with them constantly, but the time and emotional commitment she must make to CCAI's families — and the babies that would become their own — would not allow it.

In March, Lily packed her suitcase and prepared once again to say goodbye to her children. It was the second time in less than two months that they'd be separated from their mother. Snapping her suitcase shut, Lily realized that once again she was leaving behind a life that she had grown accustomed to. That life — the daily routines, the hopes and expectations — had washed away. There was no way back.

That day she wrote a prescription for survival on her calendar. Forgiveness was not yet an ingredient.

Keep on smiling in the tough reality. Believe in yourself. Be strong and self-controlled. Forget the past. Move on. Believe in God. Take care of your children. Don't give up.

⌒

The sky was slate gray on March 15 when Lily stepped down off a bus in the rural town of Yiyang in Hunan Province.

In a bright pink trench coat cinched tight at her waist, she stood out on the muddy street in a town too poor to attract tourists. The locals, in their dark, baggy clothes, froze midtask and stared. Her wavy, black hair no longer hung straight like when she left her homeland eight years before, and the shade of her lipstick matched the brilliance of her coat.

The families in Group Five exited the bus behind her, flowing out in her wake, wholly dependent on her. To anyone watching, it was obvious that the five couples and four single women, most in their forties, were Americans. Around their necks dangled cameras and video recorders, and strapped to their shoulders were bulging backpacks.

Turning to her charges, Lily led them forward. "Let's go."

She climbed the steps of a dirty, white-tiled building with a broken window gaping down from the second floor. The quiet power behind the English words she spoke, and the rundown building they were about to enter, made it clear to the locals that this woman was no tour guide. She was their leader, and she was taking them into a place few locals, never mind foreigners, ever entered.

"This is it," one of the women whispered, leaning in to her husband. They had been homing in on this moment for weeks, and they'd entrusted it to a thirty-one-year-old woman they'd known just nine months. What she would accomplish and exactly how she would pull it off remained a mystery to them.

Inside, a black veil of smoke hung in the dimness. Intermingled with the smoke was a faint smell of urine that grew stronger with each step. Lily turned back to look at them, giving them a slow smile of encouragement. Silently, she wondered what she would find in this awful place that was so cold that her soul seemed to shiver.

She had grown up at a time when Mao was bent on seizing the nation's energy for industrialization, and she knew well his declaration to his people: "No one south of the Yangtze River needs heat."

The Yiyang orphanage was one hundred miles south of China's longest and most famous river. As a child of the Cultural Revolution, Lily witnessed the suffering brought by deprivation in China, but never had she imagined children in her homeland living in a place as cold and miserable as this.

It was her second trip to China, but this one was different. In Kunming, she knew what to expect. Here, she had no idea what condition she would find these babies in. She shuddered, steeling herself for what was ahead.

It was noon when the orphanage director ushered them into a conference room. Laid out on an oval table for the foreign visitors were apples, tangerines, and Asian pears swaddled in clear plastic. At the head of the table stood Chinese officials dressed in dark suits with pressed white shirts, sweater vests, and silk ties. Graciously, Lily greeted them, bowing slightly and shaking hands. The mute Americans listened to the loud, sing-song Mandarin, understanding nothing.

They had traveled thousands of miles, boarding three planes in three days and riding a bus two hours over the rugged roads of rural China to this backwater town. Entering the dank, dark orphanage was sobering, but now, as they politely sipped lukewarm tea from formal teacups, the families began to feel a glazed-over sense of giddiness. The long wait was finally over. It was really happening.

But first there were pages and pages of adoption documents to sign. Lily translated, and they carefully wrote in English the answers to the list of questions.

"Why do you want to adopt this baby? Do you swear never to abandon or harm her?"

Each promised to care for their baby, to give her a loving home and a good education. In a seemingly endless hour, the paperwork was finished. Lily announced that it was time to pay the child-rearing fees, setting off a flurry of unzipping and unbuttoning as the families began to work through layers of clothing to retrieve money belts and wallets. Following CCAI's detailed travel instructions, each produced a stack of crisp, uncreased one-hundred-dollar bills. One of the officials collected the bills, and with the swiftness of a professional bank teller, counted out each family's three thousand dollars, bill by bill.

With all the money accounted for, the officials suddenly stood up. One made a deliberate statement to Lily in rapid-fire Mandarin, and they promptly filed out of the room. The Americans turned to her. Something didn't seem right.

In a level voice that discouraged any protest, Lily translated calmly: "It's time for lunch."

Left alone in the room, the families groaned. Lily rose to go, and reluctantly they followed. At the entrance of the orphanage, they watched the officials speed away in a sedan, the only car on the unpaved street where their daughters lived.

Hanging her head, Tish Joros trudged up the steps of the bus. It felt as if she were in a dream, and her legs wanted to ignore her brain's commands. To know their baby was somewhere in this cold, dark place but not be allowed to go to her tore at Tish. Slumping into the seat next to her husband, she remembered that day so many months earlier when they first walked into Chinese Children Adoption International's Colorado office.

The Rocky Mountains cut a jagged line into the crystal blue sky, but Tish did not notice the majesty shrinking behind her as her husband steered their car down the steep, sharp curves through the foothills toward Denver. Her eyes were closed. Silently, she repeated her simple request.

Just give us a sign.

She was a designer in a Denver floral studio, and Jim worked in the glass factory at Coors Brewing Company in Golden. Twenty years into their second marriage, they remained childless. This trip was their last chance.

A failed domestic adoption left Tish entirely ready to give up on the idea of motherhood. But a friend had heard CCAI's appeal on a Christian radio station and told the couple about it. The agency was looking for Coloradans to open their homes and hearts to Chinese orphans. The Joroses decided to try one last time.

With three other hopeful couples, they crowded at a table in CCAI's two-and-a-half-room office. The lights switched off, and a projector hummed behind them. Tish peered up at the solemn faces of six newly adopted Chinese children in Group One sitting on a couch. Instantly those faces were seared into her heart.

Later, on the way home, the woman who never cried could not stop sobbing, and the man who never stopped talking could think of nothing to say. Tish turned to her husband, wiping her wet cheeks.

"Well," she said, managing a small smile, "we got our sign."

Their decision to adopt unleashed a paper chase that might have defeated them had it not been for Lily. She told them they could do it, and they believed her. Her genius was her ability to break down into logical steps a process that others found mind-boggling. Unlike domestic agencies that could not commit to when, or even whether, couples would adopt a baby, Lily made a promise and kept it.

"Follow these steps and meet these requirements," she told them. "I will hold your hand, and you will get your baby."

Lily made it her mission to become a master of the paper maze. She brought order out of confusion, creating a system for collecting doctor reports, birth certificates and marriage certificates, getting fingerprints and personal references, filling out, notarizing and certifying forms, Fed-Exing paperwork back and forth across the country, securing approval from a social worker and the FBI. She collected the documents into a dossier, and Joshua translated everything into Mandarin.

Seven months after the Joros' dossier was sent to Beijing, they received The Call.

For Tish, it came on the floral studio's busiest day of the year — at four thirty in the afternoon on Valentine's Day. Frazzled by the annual avalanche of last-minute orders, Tish picked up the phone. Instead of a frantic husband or suitor in search of a bouquet, it was Lily.

"I have some good news for you," she sang. "You have a beautiful daughter."

For a split second, Tish was speechless. Then she cried out, "I'm a mother!"

She shot out the door into the falling snow. It was Match Day, the day she would first glimpse her daughter's face. Half an hour later at CCAI, Lily handed her the manila folder that contained her baby's picture.

"Thank you," she said, clutching it in her shaking hands and promptly turning to leave.

"Aren't you going to look?" Lily asked.

Tish shook her head.

Lily understood. She'd witnessed the awe on the faces of couples seeing the first image of the daughter they had yearned so long for. With that picture, a child was born and a dream became real.

Tish would wait. She would share that birth with her husband.

"Let me know your decision," Lily called out as Tish headed for the door.

"It's already made," she said, turning to Lily. "We accept the match. This is the child God has given us."

On an ordinary day, the drive home during rush hour would take forty-five minutes. But the snow was driving down, and her windshield wipers were laboring to sweep away the heavy flakes. Two hours up the slow, slippery highway, she pulled into her driveway. Inside, Jim had built a roaring fire. In the glow, they sat down on the floor together. Tish held her breath and opened the folder. She was surprised to see that the picture was the size of a postage stamp. They gazed into the tiny face of their daughter. Her head was tilted, and her eyes looked up expectantly.

Tish exhaled, tears shining in her eyes. "Look, Jim," she said softly, "She's saying, 'Mom, come get me.'"

It was nearly midnight when Cathay Pacific Flight 881 landed on the strange and glamorous island of Hong Kong. The lights in the cabin had been dimmed and the shades drawn during the fourteen-hour flight, but Tish and Jim could not sleep. Soon, a bus dropped the Group Five families at the Imperial Hotel. Still, the couple from the small Colorado mountain town who'd never before been out of the U.S. together were unable to fall asleep.

The next morning, the families were on a plane to Changsha. As they landed in Hunan's capital city, Jim Joros couldn't help but think that it was like flying into a crude airport in small-town America. The airport crew wheeled up a set of stairs and the passengers climbed down onto the tarmac and lined up at the plane's cargo area to collect their own luggage.

Without warning, as they sorted through the baggage, two uniformed security guards sprang toward them. Out of the line they yanked an adoptive father, his cameras swinging wildly from his neck. Leaning near his face, the guards angrily shouted orders in Mandarin. When the American responded in English, the guards became furious.

Lily spun around and leapt in front of them, shielding the American like a tigress protecting her young. Angrily, the guards accused the father of trying to sneak cameras into China to sell on the black market. Glancing at him, Lily quickly realized their mistake. They had wrongly assumed that Howard Tsuchiya, an American of Japanese descent, was one of their own countrymen.

"He is an American father," Lily said sternly, facing off with the guards. "He's here to adopt a Chinese child."

Instantly the guards backed down, chagrined to be hounding one of the Americans that the Chinese government insisted be treated with respect.

The relieved families stared at Lily. The soft-spoken woman's sudden ferocity astonished them. Slowly, the realization hit. In this foreign land, they were entirely dependent on their 120-pound leader to take care of them.

In Changsha, the streets were flooded with bicycles jockeying for space with honking buses. To the Americans, China's traffic was a disaster in the making, and collisions always seemed to be just an inch away. There didn't seem to be any regard for lanes, let alone basic traffic rules. Each time it appeared there was no way for the tour bus to avoid colliding with a biker, the families braced for the worst. When the bus finally pulled up to the Xian Jiang Hotel, they were grateful they'd made it without a wreck.

The clock in the hotel lobby said 7:57 the next morning when Lily helped the American families board the bus for Yiyang, the town where their babies lived. With her was Mr. Gu and Mr. Tan, the head of a Kunming tour company, who had agreed to help Lily.

Leaving the noisy city behind, the bus bumped along rutted roads into China's countryside, passing through gray, run-down villages on the way to Yiyang. As an attorney traveling across China, Lily had grown accustomed to seeing miles of rice paddies, where water buffalos pulled plows guided by farmers on foot in a ritual that had been carried on for thousands of years. But she had never set foot in the town of Yiyang.

Outside the bus windows, the rural tranquility was interrupted by occasional cars whizzing toward them. The vehicles would drive straight toward the bus, only to swerve away at the last second. With each near miss, the families shrieked, holding fast to the seats in front of them as they received a crash course in driving China-style. Behind the wheel of the cars were Chinese drivers who only recently had obtained their first licenses. It was the beginning of China's experimentation with capitalism, and the nation's successful, new entrepreneurs were putting cars on roads that had only seen bicycles, carts, feet, and hooves. There might have been rules for the roads, but it was obvious that Chinese drivers felt free to ignore them.

After one near collision, Lily and Mr. Tan started a sing-along to soothe the families' jangled nerves. "Rise and shine and give God the glory, glory," they sang out. The families joined in, relieved for the diversion from the traffic and their anxiety about what they would find in the orphanage.

In a melodic voice, Mr. Tan introduced the Americans to a new song, a lyrical Chinese folk song that schoolchildren learned. It was in praise of the Liu Yang, the most famous river in Hunan. He repeated the lyrics slowly, teaching the words to the American parents who would soon be caring for babies accustomed to hearing nothing but Chinese.

Jim Joros looked around at the people who had become his friends in the long hours of the past three days. As the joyful singing faded, he could see the fear creeping back onto the faces of all but Lily. Wearing sunglasses and a gold jumpsuit that Joshua and the twins had given her on her first Mother's Day, she seemed glamorous to Jim. By the time they reached Yiyang, the Americans were affectionately calling her "Hollywood."

Far from a celebrity, Lily felt like an ordinary woman who had been called to leave her young children to do a job that required her to be strong, no matter what. The only time she allowed herself to let her guard down was in the quiet of her hotel room. Even then, her only tears came when she received a fax from her children.

They had not yet learned to write. The faxes were pictures they had drawn for her, along with a note in Chinese written by their father, who wanted nothing more than to be with their mother.

We miss you.

Love, Art and Amy

It was early afternoon when the Americans left the tiny restaurant in Yiyang and returned to the empty orphanage conference room for the second time that day. There was nothing to do but wait. A few of the women reached into their purses and pulled out the tiny pictures of the daughters they'd come to claim.

Restless, Jim Joros walked to the window and peered out at the world that had surrounded his daughter for her earliest months. Across the street stood a dilapidated building, its skin peeled off and ribs exposed. Next door at an apartment building, wet clothes dangled from lines draped across the balconies of every floor. A man below pulled a wooden cart behind him, heaped with cast-off cardboard he'd scavenged. Bent over by the burden she carried, an old woman hauled baskets of produce swinging from a bamboo pole slung across her shoulders. On a rusty bicycle, a man steered a huge cart of shoes, arranged in neat rows for purchase by pedestrians passing by.

Lily was not yet in the room, and Jim wandered out in search of a bathroom. His wife and several couples followed. Like curious guests who surreptitiously snoop around when the hostess steps away, they wandered down the dark hallway. Opening the first door, Jim peered into a small, unlit room. Against one dirty wall was a single cot. On the facing wall was a row of six wooden cribs.

"Tish," he called out softly, beckoning her with his hand. "Come here."

In each crib lay a baby in a knit hat, covered by a quilt tied to the bedsides with a rope. Washed rags used as diapers hung from a clothesline strung above them. On a stool sat an old woman in a faded jacket. In her arms she held a baby engulfed in a bulky snowsuit. At the nanny's feet was an aluminum pie tin and in it were three pieces of smoking coal, the room's only source of heat. Tish started in, drawn toward the cribs, but she was stopped by a shout from the hall.

"Tish, we found her!"

"Ana?" She turned to her husband, unbelieving.

They rocketed out of the room and down the hall toward the cries of their friends. Inside another room was a nanny, her hair pulled back from her rough-skinned face. In her arms was a baby.

"*Mama? Baba?*" she asked, nodding at them.

Jim held out the tiny picture of his daughter. The nanny smiled and held up the girl. Instantly, Tish recognized Ana.

"Hi, sweet thing," she purred, taking the baby into her arms. "Hello, Ana."

She nuzzled the baby to her face, breathing in the smell of kerosene on her daughter. Arms straight out like a cross, Ana felt stiff as a board, bound up in countless layers of clothing. It was hard to imagine what had brought this child to this moment.

She would never know. Had this baby's short life included even the slightest celebration, or had it only been filled with sorrow? Tish was painfully aware of the holes that would forever exist in her daughter's story. She wondered if this precious child's first mother had given her a name, or what the mother felt knowing the child was forever leaving her life. Or whether the mother had one day returned home to discover the child was gone, taken by grandparents determined that their daughter-in-law try again to have a son.

Tish had been told that someone had carried this child away from home and left her entirely alone on the doorstep of the orphanage. Pinned to her was a note containing the only clue to her beginnings — the date she was born.

The orphanage gave her a name and a crib. A caretaker dressed her in layers of used clothing and wrapped her in a quilt, intending to protect her from the cold but binding her so tightly that she couldn't move. For months she lay there, sometimes clicking her tiny tongue on the roof of her mouth to sooth herself while she waited for a human touch. That touch came only when someone arrived to prop a bottle in her hungry mouth or to change the soiled rag stuffed between her wet legs.

Now here she was in the arms of a stranger, a woman who bore no resemblance to anyone she'd ever seen. The woman called her by yet another name in a language she'd never heard. Soon she would leave behind the country she was born in and all the people she had ever known. Holding Ana, Tish felt the weight of so much more than just a child in her arms.

"Come on," said an urgent voice from in the hallway. "They're back!"

Tish hurriedly handed Ana back to the caretaker, and the couples sprinted down the hallway back to the conference room. It was swarming again with officials. The Americans sat down again around the table, trying to conceal any sign of what they'd seen.

One by one, the babies arrived in the room in the arms of their caretakers. As each baby's name was called in Chinese, her parents rushed forward to claim their daughter.

"Yi Hui Wen," was announced.

Jim took Ana into his arms for the first time. He smiled down at her, and she stared up curiously into the bright overhead lights, a sharp contrast to the dim bulb that hung in her room. Jim gently placed Ana into the waiting arms of her mother.

Daylight was fading when the Americans filed out of the orphanage, carrying nine babies wrapped in blankets. The temperatures were near freezing, and large, cold raindrops were tumbling out of the dull sky. In the warm bus, the parents collapsed into their seats in relief.

To their surprise, Lily ordered the driver to turn off the heat. "If these babies who have lived their lives in the cold become warm too fast," she explained, "they'll get clammy and catch a cold."

Soon one baby started to whimper, then another. Before long a chorus of hungry babies had incited a flurry of action as the new parents dug into their backpacks and prepared bottles for their daughters. But the harder the babies tried to get milk from the new bottles, the more agitated they became. They did not know how to suck. A pair of scissors in hand, Lily walked up and down the aisle, clipping an X in the tip of each nipple, enlarging the hole. "In the orphanage," she told them, "mealtime was an assembly line." Cutting a big hole in the nipple made feeding time faster for overwhelmed nannies. But the babies sometimes paid a painful price for the practice. The fast-flowing milk sometimes streamed from the corners of their mouths into their ear canals, resulting in ear infections that would not heal without antibiotics — precious medicine the orphanages did not have.

Two hours later back at the hotel, Tish laid Ana on the bed. Gently, she peeled off the layers of clothing. For the first time in months, Ana was free to move her arms and legs, but instead she lay still. Tish watched and waited. Finally, Ana shifted her weight, and her arms moved. Again she was still for a moment. Then she wiggled, this time lifting her hands. She stared at them as if she'd never seen them before.

In rooms up and down the hotel hallway, parents were doing the same thing the Joroses were doing — getting to know their new daughters. They were shedding their babies' clothing, speaking in hushed tones, and doing what new parents do: carefully evaluating their child to make sure everything was as it should be. For Joan Ditges, that process quickly shifted from joy, to concern, to fear. The sinking feeling in her heart was more than enough to tell her something was not right.

It was on the morning of August 2, 1994, that Joan Ditges first saw the headline in the *Denver Post* that stopped her. "China Dolls: Abandoned baby girls bring joy to Coloradans."

A surge of loneliness welled up inside her. For years she'd wanted children, but at forty-two, she was still single. Carefully, she tore the story out and set it aside.

That afternoon, she flipped through the day's stack of mail. There was a letter from her realtor in North Carolina. Inside was a check from the closing on her house. She remembered a saying she had once read.

"In one hundred years, it will not matter what type of house I lived in or what type of automobile I drove. But the world may be different because I was important in the life of a child."

She picked up the newspaper story still sitting on the kitchen counter.

"While they may be bundles of bad luck in their homeland China, abandoned baby girls are bringing love to Colorado families," the story said.

"So far this year, eleven infant girls have been adopted with the help of Chinese Children Adoption International."

She finished reading, then she studied the newspaper picture of an eight-month-old Chinese baby girl named Mary Dumm in the arms of her mother Carolyn.

This is meant to be.

She called her parents in Florida. For several years, she'd been sending them "snow baby" Christmas ornaments that her mother treasured. It was her father, though, who received more joy from celebrating Christmas than anyone she knew.

"How would you like to trade your snow babies for a China doll?" she asked.

She told them about the newspaper story, the check in the mail, and her decision to adopt a Chinese baby. Her parents were thrilled, but cautious.

"How are you going to do this by yourself?" her father asked.

Joan was a registered nurse, and she had a secure job. There was no doubt in her mind that she could raise a child.

"I'll figure it out," she said with confidence.

"We'll do all we can to help," her father said.

She hung up, certain she was doing the right thing. Her next call was to CCAI.

The paperwork was underway that October when a phone call brought news that shattered her. Her father had died. Devastated, she collapsed back into her chair. With a jolt, she realized: *He never got to see his granddaughter.*

At that moment, she made her decision. She would honor her father and his love for Christmas by naming her daughter Holly.

Joan Ditges had been a mother for less than twenty-four hours. She and Lily gazed down at the fourteen-month-old girl whose Chinese name had been Xian Ping. The child waved her right arm freely, but Joan couldn't take her eyes off the girl's left arm. It hung motionless at her side.

Lily held out a toy to the child, and Holly grabbed it with her right hand. Then she waved another toy in front of the girl's left hand. Again, the girl reached out with her right and scooped it up. Lily took the girl's tight left fist in her hand. One-by-one, she uncurled each of the fingers. In the child's palm, she carefully placed the toy. With a thud, it fell to the floor.

Lily breathed in sharply, her heart pounding. For the first time since she'd left Colorado with Group Five, fear crept into her gut.

Carefully she listened as Joan told her what she'd seen the night before. After the long bus ride from the orphanage, she'd placed her new baby on the bed and undressed her. Holly began to cry. As the wails grew louder, the girl's back arched stiffly and her head snapped back to the right, as if she were looking over her shoulder. The sight made Joan freeze.

She had seen that twisted posture in the hospital where she was a trauma nurse. It was painful to watch. The patients who struck that contorted pose were brain-damaged. In that instant, she had recognized what was wrong.

"She has a brain injury," she told Lily, holding tight to Holly. "I'm sure of it."

Lily stared at the baby. Her instincts told her that Joan was right. "I'll find out what happened," she said.

She could see the devastation in the new mother's eyes. Lily tried to comfort her, but also prepare her. "You may want to take some time," she said gently, "to think about whether you're able to handle the demands of a special-needs child."

In her room, Lily sat down on her bed, shaking her head in disbelief. She dialed the orphanage director, trying to contain her consternation.

"Did you know Xian Ping had problems?" she asked in a level voice.

At first, the director tried to skirt the question. Lily pressed on, increasingly firm, cornering him until he confessed. The baby fell from her crib several months ago and landed on her head, but no one realized she was injured, he insisted.

Lily felt her sadness swell into raw anger.

If they knew this girl was injured, it was wrong to hide it. If they didn't realize she was hurt, it was wrong to pay so little attention that they didn't notice.

"If you want to do adoption," she told the director sternly, "you must be honest. If parents were told the truth, they might be able to prepare themselves. If they couldn't care for a handicapped child, they'd have the choice of turning down the match before they became attached."

Lily's heart ached for this girl, abandoned then injured before she even made it to a home, an ongoing tragedy no fault of her own. Lily couldn't bear the thought of leaving her behind, adding to her struggle to survive.

Gathering herself, she realized she must now focus on helping Joan come to a decision. It had to be based on the physical and financial realities of caring for a brain-damaged child, not on the emotions tearing apart a mother's heart. Lily quieted her own feelings so she could think clearly. Then the words came to her.

"You were promised a healthy child," she told Joan quietly. "This child has special needs you were unaware of. If you're able to care for the needs of a handicapped child, you can choose to keep her. If you are not, we must ask the orphanage to keep its promise."

Lily quietly left a second time to give Joan time alone to think. The new mother realized that five weeks had passed since she first received her match and fell in love with the child in the tiny picture. Now in anguish, she rocked Holly in her arms, bathing her tiny face with her own tears.

It was a soft tap that stopped her. At the door was Carol Weir, the CCAI social worker whom Lily had brought along to China. Carol was Joan's caseworker, one of the people who knew her best.

She'd visited Joan several times in Colorado to conduct the home study required for adoption. Together, they'd thumbed through the beginnings of the scrapbook Joan was creating for Holly. Pasted on the first page was the quote on making a difference in a child's life. Then came photos clipped from magazines of the Asian children that Joan had imagined her own daughter might resemble.

Most of the biographies written by those hoping to adopt were about eight pages. Joan's was thirteen, typed. Her story poured out her passion to care for others, as a nurse and a single woman who longed to be a mother. In detail, she wrote of the animals she'd taken in, including the dog with a missing front leg that she'd rescued. Joan had ended the biography stating her firm belief that God does not give you more than you can handle.

"What am I to do?" Joan implored, weeping over the child in her arms.

"You will make a tremendous difference in the life of the child you adopt," the social worker told her. "You have to decide if this will be that child."

Joan knew her capacity as a single mother, and she knew her own limits. Raising a healthy child on her own would be a difficult task, but she could do it. Alone, however, she wasn't going to be able to give a disabled child all that she needed. She didn't want to admit it to herself, but she knew she must let go of the girl she'd named in memory of her father.

The parents in Group Five who had become her friends soon filed into Joan's room, carrying their daughters with them. Before China, they had gathered for potlucks in each other's homes, sharing their dreams for the daughters they'd not yet met. Now they could see that their friend was in despair.

"There's a problem with Holly," she told them quietly, tears streaming down her face. "She fell on her head at the orphanage. Her brain is damaged."

Joan looked around the room at the pale faces of her friends.

"This is the hardest thing I've ever had to do," she continued slowly. "I'm taking Holly back to the orphanage. I'm getting another baby."

One father spoke up. "You do what you need to, Joan," he said, his husky voice cracking. "We support you. We're all in this together."

Joan silently welcomed the support, but from the pained looks on a few of the faces she could see the feelings in the room were mixed. As her travel mates left her room, she held Holly close. Never did she dream that she could feel such joy only to have it dissolve into misery.

Lily willed herself to set aside her sorrow for Xian Ping. Her duty to Joan Ditges was to convince the local officials to exchange the injured girl for a healthy child. It was the first time CCAI had ever been asked to replace a child, and she was not sure how to do it.

I know how to deal with the Chinese government. I am a lawyer. I am the daughter of a government worker. I can do this.

She made a decision. She would not merely ask the government officials to fix this. Instead, she would tell them what must happen.

"This mother is qualified to adopt a healthy child," she declared to the official in the provincial office. "She came to get a healthy child. Now, in good faith you must honor this mother's request."

Unable to argue with Lily's logic, the official agreed to the unusual request, although he admitted no mistake.

Together, Joan and Lily took the long journey back to the orphanage in Yiyang. In the front seat, Lily talked with the driver in Chinese, allowing Joan the privacy of the back seat to grieve. Joan cradled Holly in her lap, her eyes locked on the baby's angelic face.

Her tears soaked the soft bundle she clung to. To Joan, time seemed to have gone haywire. The minutes seemed to simultaneously flow by and crawl. When they pulled up to the orphanage, she had no sense if the trip had been twice as long or twice as quick. She only knew that it was the most difficult trip she had ever made.

At the dilapidated orphanage she had never expected to see again, Joan slowly placed Holly back into the arms of a nanny and the life the child had known as Xian Ping. She gave back the orphanage clothes Holly had worn, plus the new clothes she had bought for the baby. The caretaker stepped away from Joan and lowered Xian Ping onto a wooden potty chair on the floor. Joan's heart fell as her mind raced, trying to grasp what would happen next.

Suddenly the head caretaker appeared with another child in her arms. She was fourteen months old — the same age as Holly. Her mind and heart still reeling, Joan stared into the child's face.

She doesn't look at all like her.

The caretaker saw Joan's hesitation and turned to Lily.

"Have her pick one," the woman said in Mandarin.

Lily knew it was a rare offer. In Chinese adoption, it just wasn't done.

Physically, emotionally, Joan was paralyzed. She leaned over to whisper in Lily's ear. "Please," she pleaded through silent tears. "Please ask them to take Holly out. I can't bear to do this while she's watching."

Lily squatted down, lifted Xian Ping in her arms, then took her from the room. It was the last time Joan would see the child who had been her daughter for little more than a day.

A nanny showed Lily to Xian Ping's room. Lily paused and slowly lowered the child from her arms into a crib, softly touching the baby's face. Turning to the nanny, she pressed fifty dollars, all the money she had in her purse, into the woman's hand. Tears welling up, she said, "Take good care of Xian Ping."

As Lily walked back to Joan, she prayed.

Please prepare some special family to adopt this child.

In the nursery, Joan walked up and down the rows of cribs, peering into each tiny face. Never had she dreamed of having to make such a choice. Amid her frantic thoughts, Joan's eyes came to rest on a baby far younger than Holly. The girl's eyes were alert and friendly. She seemed to be smiling up at her.

"She's two-and-a-half months," the caretaker told Lily. "Her birth date is January 4."

The date jumped out at Joan. Not only was this baby younger than any China-adopted child she'd ever heard of, the girl's birthday was also just one day after Joan's father's.

This must be her. This must be my daughter.

Joan had already decided there was no way she could name this child Holly. As she pondered her options, she realized it was St. Patrick's Day. Suddenly it came to her. This baby's name would be Molly.

In the taxi, Joan nervously asked Lily to tell the driver to turn the heat on full blast and step out of the car. She laid Molly on the back seat and removed the child's clothes.

I'm not going through this again.

One by one, she examined every finger, every toe, every inch. For a long time, Joan simply gazed at Molly.

"OK," she told Lily, opening the car door. "I'm ready."

As the taxi rattled back toward Changsha, Lily was torn. This was a twist she had not prepared for. The last thing she had expected was to return to Colorado without one of the children she'd gone to get. Silently, she grieved for Xian Ping, struggling to understand why life had been so unjust to this powerless child.

Was there anything I could have done differently?

Into her mind came an ancient Chinese saying:

Bu shi yi jia ren, bu jin yi ge men.

If you don't belong to a family, you cannot go through their door.

The proverb started to make some sense.

No matter how hard I humanly try to arrange it, I cannot make someone a member of a family who is not meant for that family.

It was hours later when they arrived back in Changsha that she began to grasp her role.

My first duty is to the child. It's not in a child's best interest to be raised by parents who are not able to care for her. If a family decides not to adopt a special-needs child, it is the wrong family. My job is to talk with the family. The rest is up to God.

Back in her hotel room, Joan held Molly in her arms, but she could not stop thinking about Holly. Emotionally exhausted, she groped for her own understanding of what had happened. Slowly, achingly she decided, *Holly paved the way for Molly.*

Down the hallway, Lily lay down in the darkness of her room. The burden she carried seemed to shift as she awakened to a similar thought.

Sometimes, God may use the first child as a bridge. You can't explain it.

She picked up the phone. It was early morning in Denver, and she asked Art and Amy to play the piano for her before they left for kindergarten. As they did, the melody of the faraway piano soothed her soul.

Next she called Joshua. In his voice she heard an ache of loneliness. She told him of the heartache she'd witnessed, a day they'd never planned for when they founded CCAI. The agency had relinquished its first child and received its first replacement baby.

"I do believe God's hand was there," she said sadly. "Whatever happens, he's always teaching us something we don't see now."

Joshua took her words to heart, and they gave him a sliver of hope. The time away from Lily had been torture for him. Whenever he saw an opportunity, he threw his very being into trying to win back her trust and her love. But his exhaustive work at CCAI, the flowers and the apologies to Lily, the prayers for reconciliation — nothing seemed to work. In this moment, though, his soul leapt to know that someday he might again be with the woman he loved.

In the morning, Lily awakened to the memory of Holly's face. It haunted her. Suddenly, her plans for the day changed. She knew what she must do before she could leave this city. She must try to help Xian Ping. Quickly, she dressed and slipped outside the hotel and into a taxi.

The official at the provincial office was surprised to see the persistent Chinese woman from America back again. She told him the orphanage had offered to refund the three-thousand-dollar child-rearing fee that Joan had paid, but the mother had refused it. Gazing pointedly into the official's eyes, Lily insisted that the government order the orphanage to use the money to pay for physical therapy for Xian Ping. Moved by the determined young woman who faced him, the official gave his promise.

Lily left the office, expecting to feel better knowing that the fee would pay for five years of therapy for the child. But she didn't. The official's promise was not enough.

Lily moved forward, burying her sorrow deep inside. In time she would discover that sorrow transformed into a seed that took root and grew into a principle that Lily would live by: *CCAI leaves no child behind.* Whenever a child was replaced, CCAI would do everything in its power to see that the child received a second chance for a home or financial support to give her a better life.

Molly slept soundly in the makeshift crib in the hotel room that Joan shared with another single mother and her new daughter, who was wide awake. The baby had chicken pox, and the sores had spread into her throat. The sick girl refused her bottle. She had trouble sucking, and swallowing was more painful than hunger.

Lily knew this baby would soon be in grave danger if she didn't drink. The closest Western medicine available was a medical center near the U.S. Consulate in Guangzhou, a two-hour flight. Lily tried to sort out her options. She could not send the sick baby and her single mother by themselves, and she could not leave the rest of the families in Group Five who were awaiting the finalization of their adoption paperwork. Joan had offered to take Molly and go with them, but who would meet them in Guangzhou and help them get the medical care the baby needed?

In a moment, the answer came. Lily called Thomas He, a young English-speaking Chinese man who had helped CCAI with three groups of families in Kunming. Without hesitation, Thomas agreed to catch the next flight to Guangzhou. As Lily thanked him and hung up the phone, it struck her how valuable he was. With Thomas in Kunming, Ken Zhu in Shanghai, and Mr. Gu in Beijing, Lily was beginning to establish an innovative entity — a network of dedicated Chinese guides working directly for CCAI as local representatives. They would be Lily's eyes, ears, hands, and feet, and together they would work to get more babies out of orphanages faster.

In Guangzhou, when the two mothers and their babies landed, Thomas was standing at the gate with a sign bearing their names. He helped them navigate through the terminal and loaded them into a taxi.

At the medical center on historic Shamian Island, a doctor examined the sick infant. With medication and purple ointment to heal the red sores, he assured the new mother that her daughter would soon recover.

Sweaty and tired when they entered the atrium of the thirty-four-story White Swan Hotel, the relieved mothers soaked in the tranquil five-star hotel planted in luxurious flowers and native vegetation from famous southern China landscapes. In the center was a soothing waterfall and an ornate, gilded Chinese pavilion. Pushing through their exhaustion, they paused to take in the splendid oasis. But soon people were stopping to stare.

The White Swan was the most popular hotel for U.S. adoptive families making their mandatory last stop at the U.S. Consulate. Hotel staff and guests were accustomed to seeing the beautiful dark-haired Chinese babies with their Caucasian parents. But this baby looked like a tiny clown, with purple ointment painted over the red pox dotting her face and arms.

The mothers whisked their babies up an elevator to their room. They unpacked and headed to the hotel's Western restaurant, with its huge windows overlooking the busy Pearl River. Scanning the first English menu she had seen in nearly two weeks, Joan placed her order: Cheeseburger and fries. And ketchup. It was like manna from heaven.

Soon Thomas was back at the busy airport, picking up Lily and the other families in Group Five. Wrapping up the final steps of their journey, the families arrived at the American Consulate at their appointed time.

An official slowly reviewed Molly's passport as Joan held her breath. He looked up, pointing to Holly Ditges' birthday. That would make her fourteen months old, he noted. It didn't take a genius to see that Molly was barely bigger than a newborn.

"If there's anything you'd like to discuss or adjust," the official said, his voice deliberate, "now would be the time."

Inside Joan felt the rising panic. Her baby's birth date was wrong and so was her name.

I'm not risking anything now.

She steadied herself and looked directly at the official.

"No," she said with certainty. "There's nothing."

When the exhausted families stepped into Denver's airport, they were greeted with the bright lights of a local TV news camera and shouts from the friends and relatives there to meet the newly formed families. Standing in front were Joshua and the twins, holding a huge, white banner with two words in red, the color for good luck in China: "Welcome Home." As cameras flashed around her, Lily folded her children into her arms.

On the evening news that night, Channel 9 reported: "An adoption agency in Denver is turning tragedy into joy, changing the lives and the fortunes of babies forever."

"How does it feel to make such a change in a child's life?" the reporter asked, holding a microphone in the face of one of the mothers.

"It's great," Joan Ditges answered, looking down at Molly. Then her smile faded. "But it feels sad that there are other ones over there. It's hard to see them, and then leave them."

In her backyard, all around Lily was fresh growth and new life as springtime washed over the Rockies. But deep inside her was a constant ache. Watching the twins play gave her comfort, even though the amount of time she spent away from them tugged at her conscience. A pool of emotions swirled inside her: pride at what CCAI had accomplished; fear and anger for the babies' predicament overseas in China; anxiety for the months she knew she would spend in China away from her treasured children; and pain over the crisis in her marriage.

Into her mind came the Bible verse that her friends the Laymans had offered to comfort her: *We know that in all things God works for the good of those who love him, who have been called according to his purpose.*

Her father had gently tried to ease her suffering by offering another thought: The pain is great now, but let some time go by.

But it was the advice she received from a counselor recommended by Dr. Covell that started the slow thaw in her heart.

You cannot be at peace until you open yourself to forgiveness. If you are not willing to leave what happened to the past, it will always come back to haunt you. It's your choice whether to continue to suffer or to forgive. God gives you that choice.

Babies in the Zhuzhou orphanage; 1992

Joshua and Dr. Ralph Covell
in Kunming; 1994

Lily with Mr. Gu; 1995

Joan Ditges with Molly; 1995

Local TV station filming
Molly Ditges; 1995

Patti and Darrell Doering
with Kelsey; 1995

Lily holding lilies and
baby Lily in front of
the Lily Hotel; 1995

Dr. Liu Xiang Guo with
David and Rebecca
Blank and Laura; 1996

Joshua, Lily, Amy, and Art with Dr. Jack and
Liz Layman; 2002

Lily at the dedication of the second Lily Orphan
Care Center in Fuling; 2002

Arriving in Denver
with Anna; 2004

Chinese Children Charity's first
donation of formula; 1995

Hao bao bao. Hao bao bao.

Precious baby. Precious baby.

TEN

I WILL NOT LET YOU DIE

April 1995

GROUP SIX: XIAOSHAN, ZHEJIANG PROVINCE

The boats floating through the shimmering mist of West Lake dazzled the American families when they first arrived in Hangzhou, a captivating city one hundred twenty miles southwest of Shanghai that was known for its beautiful women. But this was different. Stepping over the threshold into a strange, murky world, they were now behind the closed doors of an orphanage in the nearby city of Xiaoshan.

As their names were called, the families stepped forward with open arms to embrace their daughters. Holding them and trying to absorb every wondrous detail of their children for the first time, the families now tentatively trailed the voices of Lily and the orphanage director down a dim hallway. They were going to see the room where their children had lived the earliest months of their lives. They knew so little of the children's histories that the families were content to interrupt their dreams of the future to step, even for a moment, into their girls' past.

Fracturing their worlds, a muffled cry escaped from behind a closed door. The cry was followed by another, this one more piercing. Alarmed, the parents looked wide-eyed to their leader. Lily stopped at the door, and the families halted behind her. Putting her ear to the door, she listened to the

175

cries. Hesitantly, she reached out to the doorknob. She turned it, but the door would not open.

"Why is it locked?" she asked, turning to the director, who was now walking back to the group.

"It's a room for handicapped children," he replied, his cheerful face suddenly solemn.

"Who takes care of them?"

"We feed them at meal time. Then we lock them in to keep them safe."

Skeptical, Lily stared hard at the man. His eyes had turned stony. The cries behind the locked door grew more insistent.

"When is the next meal?" Lily pressed. "Can you open the door so we can see them?"

"No," he said flatly. "It's nap time."

Without another word, he wheeled around and stalked down the hall.

Lily paused. She knew she should follow him, but that door and the voices beyond it dragged at her heart. The families looked at her, holding their babies close. She glanced at Mr. Gu, who had flown in from Beijing to help her. He shook his head. Lily pushed the cries out of her mind, commanding her feet to move, to follow the director. Slowly, the families trailed behind her.

It was the first time she heard — but did not see — what a British TV report labeled the orphanage "Dying Room." But she did not need to see it. The cries from behind the closed doors echoed inside her and haunted her.

Hangzhou, Zhejiang Province

A few days later, the bus pulled up to a well-maintained building that was far larger than the other orphanages Lily had visited. By the looks of the beautiful green grounds and the handsome stone statues of mothers with children, it appeared this orphanage in Hangzhou was well funded.

The two families from Group Six who received their daughters from this orphanage had returned to see the nursery. But walking from the formal conference room into the babies' room was like leaving a world of color and light and entering a place of bleak darkness. Like the poorest rural orphanages, the closer they got to the nursery the stronger the stench of soiled diapers.

The babies on their backs in the cold, messy nursery were thin and dirty. Some were severely handicapped, desperately in need of treatment. As Lily walked among the children, she could not take her eyes off one girl, whose ballooned head was massive compared with that of a healthy infant.

Victoria Lierheimer, an adoptive parent, froze at the sight. "It's water on the brain," she whispered to Lily.

She knew because she was born with it. Her father had saved his daughter's life by creating a needle technology to drain the water from her dangerously enlarged head.

"This baby will die if we don't do something," she said, her voice urgent.

Lily approached the orphanage principal, who was also a doctor. Respectfully, she explained to the director the needle routinely used in America to treat babies born with this life-threatening condition.

"There is no such technology in China for orphans," the director replied firmly.

"If it's money, tell us," Lily said, her eyes pleading. "We can help."

Emphatically, the doctor shook her head. The conversation was closed and the tour was over.

As the families shuffled back on to the bus, one distraught mother asked Lily, "What can we do?"

Lily could see where the money was being spent in this place and why. The orphanage officials were creating a facade by maintaining a nice building and receiving room for important visitors. She saw that the leaders who presented themselves as loving in reality cared very little about these children.

"What is needed," she told the mother, "is a change in leadership."

As the bus rumbled away, she stared out the window at the well-manicured grounds. It all seemed so hopeless.

I'm working as fast as I can to get them out. There's no time left to help those left behind. But who else will help? They have no family, no power, no authority. Yet someone must speak for them.

It was beyond Lily's imagination at the time, but her frustration would one day become the transforming power this orphanage needed. In five years this place of dread would become a place of hope, a place with a new look, a new feel, a new attitude, and a new name: the Lily Orphan Care Center.

Perhaps sensing that Lily would one day leave her mark on this place, the families later presented their leader with a bouquet.

There, before leaving their hotel, Lily posed for a picture. In one arm she held the lilies, in the other she held a baby named Lily, and behind her was the *Bei He Hua* — the Lily Hotel.

~

MAY 1995

GROUP SEVEN: CHANGSHA, HUNAN PROVINCE

A shy little girl sat quietly next to Lily. The paperwork said Guo Lan was four years old, but in fact this child was six. When she first arrived two years earlier at the Changsha orphanage, the malnourished girl was already four. But Guo Lan was so small that her caretakers wrongly guessed her age was two.

Guo Lan was the oldest child to be adopted through CCAI so far, and the first able to tell her own story. In a world where families had to learn to embrace the mystery of their daughters' pasts, Lily knew that Guo Lan's journey would always feel different.

Lily spoke softly to the child in Mandarin, and after a while encouraged her to remember back to the time she first came to the orphanage. Guo Lan hesitated, staring at her shoes. But Lily's patience and warmth set the girl at ease, and eventually her quiet words bore them back, away from the bench they sat upon, away from the orphanage.

Father took me to the park to play. We had fun together, playing.
When it was time to leave, he said, "Let's stop by the toilet."
He took me to the ladies' side. "When you're finished," he said,
   "wait outside for me."
I waited and waited. My father never came.
Later, someone saw me crying and took me to the orphanage.
I blame myself. I didn't wait long enough.

Guo Lan lowered her eyes, silent. Lily tried hard to hold back her own tears, putting her arm around the small girl and nestling Guo Lan into her side.

As she felt Guo Lan's breathing against her, Lily refused to lament the girl's past. She forced herself to focus on the child's hopeful future. Not all that long ago, an American had spent time volunteering in the orphanage. The more time she spent there, the more she was drawn to Guo Lan. When the woman returned to the States, she carried with her the memory of the precious girl, and she shared it with her friends. Now it was some of those friends, Dennis Wagner, a pastor, and his wife, Brenda, a school teacher, who were bringing their new daughter home to America. Their story and Guo Lan's were now intertwined.

~

ZHUZHOU, HUNAN PROVINCE

After a four-hour drive from the orphanage in Yueyang back to Changsha, the joyous new parents in Lily's care settled into their hotel rooms with their long-awaited daughters. The nine babies were tiny but alert.

When she was confident there were no crises to tend to, Lily slipped away on a journey of her own. She wanted to check in on some babies in the Zhuzhou orphanage who were waiting for the next group of CCAI families to arrive in Hunan.

An hour later, Lily was following the orphanage director up the stairs into another cold, unlit room. Along one gray wall was a row of wooden cribs, each home to two bundled babies. The infants, all girls, were still. Tiny knit hats shrouded their heads, and heavy quilts were pulled up to their noses. Their flat, dark eyes stared up at the ceiling.

Lily lifted one of the tiny infants into her arms. She felt more like a forgotten rag doll than a child, her thin body limp, her dirty face listless. Gently, Lily swayed with her, whispering, *"Hao bao bao. Hao bao bao."* Precious baby. Precious baby.

As a mother, she knew that babies could be coaxed to smile if they are warm, dry, and well-fed. But these babies were cold, wet, and hungry. They lived in a place with no heat or hot water. They drank from bottles propped into their mouths by caretakers too busy to hand-feed them or change the dirty diapers they lay in.

Pulling her camera from her purse, Lily took snapshots of each child. The pictures would help sustain their future parents waiting in America for the day they could hold their daughters.

Satisfied with the pictures she had, she left the babies and walked down the hallway to the bathroom. From the corner of her eye, she glimpsed something on the floor.

Naked on the cold tile lay a tiny girl. Her black hair was chopped short, her eyes half-open. The bones of her rib cage poked through the skin of her birdlike body. Lily guessed the toddler weighed no more than twelve pounds. Her clenched fists were at her side, and her thin legs curled to her chest. Horrified, Lily knelt down. She could barely feel the child's weak breath.

She dashed back to the babies' room for a blanket and a bottle, crying out to a caretaker, "Who is that girl in the bathroom? Why was she left on the cold floor with no clothes?"

Flying back to the girl, Lily touched the child's hands. She shuddered when she felt the girl's cold skin. She leaned in closer. The girl was no longer breathing.

Everything but the girl's lifeless body seemed to melt away as Lily felt a wave crash over her. Collapsing on the floor beside the child, she cried out in agony. She wrapped her shaking arms around the girl and broke down, weeping like a mother who had lost her own baby.

Why, why did this have to happen?

The caretaker stared at the grieving young woman until Lily finally rose, drained.

Why didn't I get here a few minutes earlier? Perhaps I could have saved her.

Slowly, she walked out of the orphanage, leaving the girl behind. On the way back to Changsha, she stared out the window, wrestling with the fragility of the lives of the children she was trying to rescue.

Sometimes we are too late.

∿

EARLY JUNE 1995
DENVER, COLORADO

Lily bent over the backpacks in the twins' room, showing Art and Amy how to pack the clothes they would need for their first trip to China. The twins couldn't wait for their inaugural flight overseas with their mother, and Lily's parents were eager to go home for a visit. In Beijing, Lily would say goodbye to the twins and travel on to the province of Anhui with Group Nine. Art and Amy would take the train with their grandparents to Shenyang, then travel by car to Fushun, the town where their mother and father had met.

It had been six months since Joshua had left. He had thrown himself into winning her forgiveness, but it had taken Lily that long to grieve the loss that had for so long seemed unbearable. She knew it was time to forgive Joshua. It was impossible to keep pretending to be a loving couple and work together with no forgiveness in her heart. Until there was forgiveness, she knew they could not work side by side in peace. She made the conscious choice to forgive, but not forget.

Joshua recognized the magnitude of Lily's step and was thankful for the slow softening of her heart. With hope taking root, he vowed to himself to keep working to rebuild the foundations of their fragile relationship.

∿

JUNE 20
GROUP NINE: BANGBU, ANHUI PROVINCE

There were nine babies in Group Nine, nearly all healthy. As she walked among the families in the moments after their daughters arrived, Lily concentrated on Kelsey Doering. She lifted the baby's thin hand. The bones of the girl's slender fingers protruded from her skin like twigs.

At nearly five months, the severely malnourished child was smaller than most newborns. Lily guessed she weighed four, maybe five pounds. She couldn't believe this baby was still alive after the draining four-hour trip from her orphanage in Bangbu to Group Nine's hotel in Hefei, the impoverished provincial capital of Anhui.

Even more astonishing, Lily saw absolutely no fear in the eyes of Kelsey's parents when, on Father's Day, the dangerously weak baby was placed in their arms. Until that moment, Patti and Darrell Doering, both thirty-five, had never been parents.

The black fluff of the baby's hair stuck straight up, new growth from the buzz cut the orphanage gave her for good luck. Her pale cheeks were sunken, but her dark eyes were lively, almost impish. Her new parents could see that she was puny, but it didn't even occur to them that she might not make it.

Unlike parents of underweight babies in other groups that year, the Doerings did not pull Lily aside to ask if their tiny daughter was in danger. Compared to Group Nine's biggest baby, a chubby, nineteen-pound girl from the orphanage in Hefei, Kelsey Doering seemed near starvation. Lily was worried they might lose her.

"Do you have any concerns?" Lily asked the Doerings, gently probing.

They both shook their heads, gazing adoringly at their new daughter.

Lily was taken aback. "Are you worried about how small she is?" she continued, trying to help the couple understand the gravity of their baby's condition.

"She's our daughter," Patti said lovingly. "She'll be fine."

Lily tried again. She wanted them to know they had a choice about whether to keep this sickly baby. At the same time she knew if the Doerings didn't take Kelsey, this baby would surely die.

"Are you OK to take care of her?" Lily said.

"She just needs a lot of tender, loving care," Patti said cheerfully.

Lily knew that a child this small who could survive in an orphanage for five months had the will to live, a strong mind, and a strong body. She'd watched malnourished babies in orphanages fighting for their lives, and she'd seen how tough and aggressive they could be. They were fighters who would not die easily. But this skeleton of a child was the tiniest orphanage baby Lily had ever seen.

The nannies wanted Kelsey's orphanage clothes back, so Patti followed them into a room to undress her daughter. On the baby's bottom was a mark. The caretaker explained that the girl was so dehydrated they'd taken her to the hospital. Instead of inserting an IV into the veins of her head or her shrunken hand, the doctors placed the needle into what was left of the fatty tissues of her bottom.

Kelsey refused to take the orphanage formula, a sweet, watery liquid that tasted to Patti like pure sugar. The baby's hunger drove her to cry. Patrolling the hotel hall on the floor where the families stayed, Lily heard wailing from the Doerings' room.

She tapped on the door. "Can I help?"

Darrell opened the door, surprised. They hadn't called for Lily, but she seemed to appear when they needed her most. Kelsey was sobbing, inconsolable.

Lily could see the strain in the face of the new father.

"Let me see if she'll sleep for me," Lily said, her voice kind.

Lily wrapped a baby blanket tightly around the girl's thin body, enveloping her like a cocoon the way she'd seen nannies swaddle babies in the orphanages. The binding gave the infants the feeling of being embraced, a sense of security that the nannies had no time to give.

She lifted up Kelsey, and rocked the distraught infant in her arms. Softly, she sang a Chinese folk song, firmly patting the baby's side in a steady one-two-three-four beat. It was a secret she learned from her father, who long ago used it to soothe his first grandson.

Mesmerized by the rhythm of Lily's methodic pats, Kelsey slowly relaxed into sleep.

Patti was in awe.

"There's no baby I cannot get to sleep," Lily said, smiling reassuringly. She lowered the sleeping baby into the crib.

But soon Kelsey was awake again, crying even louder. Hearing her screams, Lily returned to the room to try to comfort her. But she barely lulled the baby back to sleep when Kelsey awoke again with a start. This time her sobs were uncontrollable.

"Kelsey may be sicker than you think," Lily said gravely. "You must think about whether you're able to take care of her."

Her words were sobering. But even then, it did not occur to the Doerings that keeping this severely malnourished baby could mean returning home empty-handed. Their decision was final, they told Lily. This baby was their daughter, no matter what happened.

"She's the right one for us," Patti said. "God will take care of her."

Before they ever received her picture, they prayed that Kelsey would be cared for at the orphanage and that God would help them to be good parents.

"We can do it," Darrell told his wife. "We'll get through this."

Lily's eyes moved from the Doerings to the wailing child. In that tense moment, she made a silent vow to Kelsey Doering.

I will not let you die.

Each time Kelsey cried, Patti walked her around the room. She took deep breaths to calm her own raw nerves, until she could no longer bear the screams. Then Darrell took over.

For the coming days, Lily kept vigil over the struggling couple. When she saw that the baby's crying was too much for them, she told the Doerings it was time to take a break. She bundled Kelsey up and took the baby to her own room. For the next few hours, she did all she could think of to console the ailing baby.

Ten precarious days later at the medical center in Guangzhou, Lily was relieved to learn that Kelsey had gained some weight, although the tiny baby was still fragile.

Hang in there. You're almost home.

On June 25, as the plane touched down in Denver, Lily felt a tremendous weight lift from her chest. It was the end of her fifth trip to China in six months. Never had she been so relieved to safely deliver a group back home.

Kelsey was still dangerously thin. Lily had seen malnourished babies flourish once they settled in with their new families in America. But even at home, Kelsey refused to eat. The pediatrician ran tests, but could not find what was wrong with the girl.

The day Kelsey's temperature spiked to 104, the Doerings took her to The Children's Hospital. A menacing red rash had crept across her body. First the doctors ordered a painful spinal tap, then tests on the baby's heart. Finally, for the first time, the Doerings received a diagnosis. Their daughter had cytomegalovirus, a virus that could cause serious illness when passed during pregnancy from the infected mother to her unborn baby.

"Without treatment," the doctor said, "a baby born with it can die."

Children's Hospital pumped Kelsey full of antibiotics, and the Doerings found by trial-and-error a soy-based formula she would eat. Lily was thrilled and relieved when she learned that Kelsey was finally thriving.

In August, the families in Group Nine gathered with their daughters for their first reunion in Denver. No one even recognized the plump, smiling Doering baby who had heroically defied the odds.

Later that year, China's Civil Affairs Ministry publicly estimated that five hundred thousand abandoned children lived in its orphanages, although World Vision claimed the number was closer to a few million. When she heard a horrifying report that the mortality rate for infants in their first six months in a Chinese orphanage was 36 percent, all Lily could do was say a prayer of gratitude. Kelsey Doering had escaped. She had fought — and won.

~

JUNE 25
GROUP TEN, HANGZHOU, ZHEJIANG PROVINCE

At the Lily Hotel in Hangzhou, a family in Group Ten stood beside Lily, watching their new daughter scamper down the hall. They could count the hours they'd been with the little girl, and for the most part all was going well. But they were worried whether everything was all right, mainly because the toddler had a large, broad forehead.

"Do you think she might be retarded?" the mother asked Lily quietly.

Smiling, Lily reassured them that their daughter was healthy. "Look at my huge forehead," she told them, "and I turned out fine."

The parents gazed at their daughter anxiously. Art and Amy chased after the girl, each taking one of her hands. They skipped down the hallway, their peals of laughter bouncing through the hall as the trio tumbled down together.

It was the first time the twins had traveled with adoptive families. Lily had picked them up from her parents in Shenyang and flown them more than a thousand miles south to Hangzhou, where they'd joined Group Ten. Art and Amy were only five and a half, but Lily was confident she could watch over them while caring for the ten adoptive families on the trip.

Now it was Art and Amy who were helping her. Up and down the hall they ran, swinging the giggling girl between them. The child's parents soon were laughing along with the kids; their worries faded from thought.

But some of the babies from the Yiwu orphanage were so sick with fever and pinkeye that Lily had to take them to see a doctor. Having grown up in the United States, Art and Amy didn't know what to expect when they tagged along. Inside the dark and dingy hospital, they waited for hours alone in the lobby for their mother, desperately slapping at the swarms of mosquitoes that kept biting them.

To Lily's relief, the doctors were able to help, and the babies' fevers broke in time for Group Ten to head for Guangzhou.

⌢

NOVEMBER

DENVER

Stepping off the scale, Lily sighed. She had traveled to her homeland nine times in 1995. Before her first trip with Group Four to Kunming, she weighed 120 pounds. Now after coming home from Chongqing with Group Fifteen, the scale barely hit 96.

Joshua had been working ever-increasing hours at the office to keep up with the agency's spiraling growth. For all the times he reached out for her forgiveness, Lily had seen him only when necessary — at the office or at home when he picked up Art and Amy. They had attended CCAI events together, but in the group photo taken at a reunion of adoptive families, they were not standing next to each other. It was typical of the photos they were in that year — together, but apart.

Gone more than half the year, Lily was exhausted, although she did not show it. She'd worked as hard and as fast as she humanly could. Her goal had been to retire from CCAI after placing one hundred babies. By year's end, she had brought home one hundred and forty Chinese children, seven times the number of CCAI babies placed in 1994. But to Lily, it was not enough.

She had set foot in just a fraction of the orphanages scattered across China, but what she had seen was impossible for her to shake. She couldn't bear to think of the suffering children left behind. On her own, she knew there was little she could do. Joshua was the one who could help her.

"No matter how hard I work, I can't bring them all home," she told him one day.

"I know," he said. "But I wish we could."

"They can't wait for us to find them a home. We have to do something right now ... before they die. We have to feed them."

Joshua knew then what his next task at CCAI was. He must help China's abandoned babies by using the fundraising gifts that got the young couple all the way from China to Denver.

He decided to start with those who were most motivated to help — CCAI's adoptive families. They were the ones he'd often heard say, "I can only bring one baby home. What can I do for the rest?"

Buy formula.

With a passion, Joshua went to work raising money to feed orphanage babies in the northeastern province of Hebei. The four thousand dollars he raised would over the next decade become a fund of four million dollars to help children in China's orphanages. But it was that very first donation that changed the agency's mission and reopened the closed door to Lily's heart. It was no longer a traditional nine-to-five adoption agency focused solely on creating new families. It was now a place where the founders worked day and night to give new life to orphans about to be adopted — and those left behind.

Out of the couple's broken marriage had come what felt like the birth of another child — Chinese Children Adoption International. And as the proud parents, Lily and Joshua committed themselves to doing all they could to nurture what was growing into a massive orphan rescue mission from one side of the world to the other.

The things we lose have a way of coming back to us,
just not in the way we expected.

ELEVEN

INTO THE FLAMES
1996

On July 29, at the height of southern China's sweltering summer, an unexpected call interrupted Lily's packing. She was in Hong Kong, about to fly back to America after leading Group Thirty-Three to Fujian Province. Away from home for nearly two weeks, she was yearning to see Art and Amy. The twins had finished first grade, and their summer vacation would soon be over. She would be in Denver just long enough to pick them up and all head back to Guangxi Province with the families in Group Thirty-Four.

Since she'd arrived in the United States nearly ten years earlier, she'd longed to make this journey back to Guilin, the heavenly mountain town where her mother had grown up. It had been twenty years since she had last seen the grandmother who had helped raise her when she was a small girl. Lily would unite the American families with daughters, then take Art and Amy to visit Grandma Liu.

"Lily," came the urgent voice on the phone. "You can't go back to America."

It was Mr. Gu.

"Why? What's wrong?" she shot back, fear cutting into her.

"You have to come to Changsha right away," he said. "It's our babies … they're very sick. The orphanage won't let them go."

Mr. Gu had become CCAI's top in-China lieutenant. By now he had helped the agency deliver more than one hundred and fifty babies to American families. Lily knew he would never ask her to come to Changsha unless the situation was dire.

That day, he and Ken Zhu, another trusted CCAI representative, had entered the white, four-story orphanage with the Group Thirty-One families in high spirits. They were finally just moments from holding their babies. The orphanage officials ushered them into a conference room, then quickly pulled the CCAI reps back outside. As the men spoke in hushed voices, the parents stared anxiously, straining to hear the words they could not comprehend.

The minutes seemed to drag on. Finally, the officials stepped back in the room, their faces grim. Mr. Gu struggled to compose himself, but dread was visible on his face.

He opened his mouth to speak, but his voice broke. Overcome with emotion, he turned away.

"What? What's wrong?" the parents demanded.

Ken stepped up. In his mind, he could hear Lily's voice. "First, you must remain calm. If you panic, the parents will panic too."

"Your babies," he said in a strong, steady voice. "Have muscles."

"Muscles?" asked a parent, confused.

"Not muscles," Ken said, searching for the right pronunciation. "Measles."

Despite their fear, several parents smiled nervously.

"I am sorry," he said, his voice tender with compassion. "But some of you will not be allowed to take your babies today."

Gasps rippled through the room.

Torrential summer rains had flooded the banks of the Yangtze River to the north, damaging an orphanage and leaving its children homeless. The Changsha orphanage had taken them in, unaware that the babies had measles. The infected children were placed in empty cribs in the nursery, right next to babies destined for adoption. Soon the measles had spread to the children in Group Thirty-One.

Most of China was not immunized against measles, and the risk of infection was high. Allowing the contagious babies to leave the orphanage would be too dangerous — for the babies and those they came in contact with. Seven of the babies in Group Thirty-One were quarantined, leaving just four who would be allowed to go with their parents right away.

David Blank, a young pediatrician in his thirties, and his wife, Rebecca, a registered nurse, were the first to understand the seriousness of the situation. The couple knew there were two types of measles. The first was Rubella, the "easy" or "three-day" measles not seen in the U.S., where Americans are vaccinated. The second was Rubeola, the "hard" measles, which is considered far more serious. These babies had Rubeola, and David knew from experience that it could be fatal. A medical resident during an outbreak of Rubeola in America, he remembered that two infected children had died.

Shocked, the parents sat silent, waiting to hear which babies would be allowed to leave. One by one, four babies were placed into the arms of their relieved parents. Then, an official told Mr. Gu the families must return to their hotel. The empty-handed parents stared in disbelief.

In a chorus that rose all at once, they begged to see their babies. Mr. Gu had regained his composure, and the voice of the soft-spoken man turned tough. With quiet authority, he told the officials these parents would not leave without first seeing their daughters. The officials protested, but Mr. Gu refused to give in, and at last they relented.

To the families, this ancient Hunan capital on the dirty Xiang River, with its three thousand years of recorded history, was a place most Americans would not set foot unless they had come for a baby. Now, on the day when they had anticipated joy, they were clouded with fear.

They filed out of the air-conditioned conference room, following the officials to the nursery where their babies now lived. The stifling heat and the stench of rotten diapers made it hard to breathe.

Seeing their sick daughters for the first time, the families felt little relief. Red spots covered the babies' bodies, and their faces were flush with fever. Above them, black flies buzzed through the air.

Frustration simmered inside Tom Ponrick, who had traveled from Colorado with his wife to realize their dream for a baby. Here they were in a foreign country where they didn't speak the language, and now nothing was going as planned.

A caretaker placed Liu Fan in Leslie Ponrick's arms. In the moment that she'd always imagined would be thrilling, she was consumed with worry about her baby's well-being.

As Tom videotaped, he could see that Liu Fan was worn out, but she held her head up and looked curiously at the strangers. Her face was somber, but he was encouraged that she looked as good as she did.

"They're going to be OK," he said, trying his best to sound upbeat.

Rebecca Blank felt the hot forehead of the baby who was now her daughter. Laura was feverish, but her eyes were alert. The Blanks, parents of two sons, had known they were taking a big risk by adopting a daughter in China. But from the beginning they had felt a sense of providence about this baby. Now they could think only of how they could help Laura and the other feverish babies wilting in the hot orphanage room.

"When can you come to Changsha?" Mr. Gu asked Lily, his voice urgent. She knew he was scheduled to fly out to unite another group of parents with their babies.

"I'll be there as fast as I can. How are the parents doing?"

"They're upset, but they know we're doing what we can for the babies," he said.

"Tell them I'm coming," she said, trying to be reassuring.

But inside, she felt fear strangling her heart.

What if they die before I get there?

Lily picked up the phone and dialed Colorado. Joshua was grateful to hear his wife's voice. They had been working at CCAI as if nothing had happened between them, with Lily overseeing adoptions as executive director and Joshua building the Chinese Children Charity Fund as development director. To the few people who knew of the strain between them, Lily had explained, "We must bear the burden of brokenness to work together to build new families."

Now Joshua was awaiting her return to Denver with renewed anticipation. Before his wife had flown to Fujian with Group Thirty-Three, she had taken a major step toward reconciliation. After a year and a half, Lily had finally agreed to let him return home.

Grateful to move back in with his family, Joshua had leapt into the role of serving them — caring for the twins, cooking and cleaning, relieving Lily of household duties so she could stay up late into the night answering calls from the agency's representatives in China and advising them how to solve each new problem the families faced.

His wife soon would be home, and his family would be together again for a few days before Lily flew back to China.

"I can't come home," she told him.

"What?" he stammered as he felt his anticipation sink. "Why?"

"I have to fly to Changsha. Mr. Gu just called and told me our babies have measles."

"Measles? Are they OK?" he asked, grasping the gravity of Lily's decision.

"They're quarantined, so I have to go be with them," she said. "You'll have to send Art and Amy without me."

"Alone? But they're only six," Joshua said, trying to wrap his mind around the thought of his kids flying halfway around the world with no parent at their sides.

"They can do it. You can send them with Group Thirty-Four."

"OK," Joshua said, trying to take in the sudden turn of events. "Don't worry. I'll figure it out. You just get to those babies."

The next afternoon, Tom Ponrick videotaped his wife as she held Liu Fan. Their baby seemed a bit better, although the tiny girl felt more like a newborn in her mother's arms than a child nine months old. When Leslie fed her a bottle, the baby drank it all.

"She sure has a good appetite," Tom quipped optimistically.

Laura Blank lay against her mother's chest, her eyes half closed. Missionaries who'd been volunteering at the orphanage had told Rebecca they'd nicknamed her cheerful thirteen-month-old Joy-Joy. But Joy-Joy was no longer smiling. Her head drooped, and she could not hold herself upright.

The parents focused their entire being on their daughters, knowing that their visits would be limited. Their first times with their babies were so different than they had imagined during their months of waiting. But they knew they would go to any length to help their daughters. When the officials announced the visit was over, the parents reluctantly said goodbye to their babies and slowly filtered out of the room. But the Blanks held back. They were determined to find a way to stay.

It was Mr. Gu who helped persuade the skeptical officials that a pediatrician and a nurse could help the overworked nannies care for the sick children. Working alongside two caretakers that day, the couple changed diapers, fed the babies bottles, and took temperatures.

Two to a crib, the babies lay on straw mats intended to relieve the oppressive heat. All of them had high fevers. Without even thinking to ask permission, David Blank quietly started giving the babies Tylenol to try to break their fevers. When a caretaker saw what the doctor was doing, she stopped him. Scolding the doctor, she insisted that allowing a fever to run its course would kill the infection. Knowing that he already was lucky to even be in the room with the children, David backed off.

Six hours after they'd arrived, Rebecca and David left the orphanage. Back at the hotel, David tried to reassure the anxious parents that they were doing what they could to care for their sick babies. The drained couple then returned to their hotel room, and sitting near the still-empty crib, they did the only other thing they knew to do: They prayed.

Returning to the orphanage the following day, three of the babies had improved. But four others had raging fevers. Laura Blank's temperature was 104.5, and Liu Fan's hit 105. Both were dehydrated and listless.

Still, the officials refused to use medication to break the babies' fevers. Instead, a caretaker gave each one a penicillin shot. Surprised by the sharp prick of the needle, Laura let out a small cry. David Blank sighed, knowing the unnecessary injection — delivering an antibiotic — was no cure for a viral disease, not to mention the fact it introduced the risk of infection from a potentially dirty needle.

He did not protest the penicillin itself, but it was impossible not to speak up when he saw the nurse reusing needles taken from a steamer. He was grateful when she agreed to use the bag of disposable sterile syringes he offered her.

Panic started to take hold when Leslie Ponrick saw the distress her baby was in. Liu Fan could no longer hold her head up. Leslie cradled the baby's head in the crook of her elbow and cupped her hand under the child's bottom. Liu Fan felt like a rag doll.

A caretaker approached Leslie and handed her a steaming hot medicine that looked to her like tar. Leslie glanced at her husband. She dabbed a finger into the thick slime to take a taste before feeding it to Liu Fan. It was horrible. Reluctantly, whispering that she was sorry, she did as she was told and gave the medicine to the baby.

Increasingly, the small, hot room was filled with coughing and wheezing. David had expected some respiratory distress, a complication of measles, but it seemed that with each moment, the babies' breathing became more labored — and more alarming.

This time, as they had to leave the babies behind, Rebecca Blank wept. Worry had eroded into cold fear. Her mind could not get past how quickly the babies' conditions were deteriorating.

Late that night in the orphanage, Rebecca's fears were realized. In addition to measles, the babies now had pneumonia. When caretakers saw the four sickest babies gasping for air, they realized these girls were not just ill; they were fighting to survive. They bundled up the wheezing babies and took them to Changsha Children's Hospital, hoping for the best, but fearing the worst.

The families rushed through breakfast after they found out their daughters had been transferred to the hospital during the night. They were desperate to be with them, but they had no idea what to expect.

Accustomed only to U.S. hospitals, the crude conditions in the Changsha facility floored the Americans when they finally arrived. Puddles of rainwater stood on the floor below open windows in a hallway reeking of urine. The grinding whine of generators grew louder as the lights flickered, dimmed for a split-second, and then surged brighter once again. Beds bearing small children lined the walls of the hall. In one, a nearly lifeless boy no older than five lay on a cloth mattress with no sheets or pillow. On the floor, his distraught parents squatted next to him, trying to feed him a bit of green melon. Each rattled breath seemed to be his last.

"He looks like he's dying," Rebecca Blank whispered to her husband as they followed the group.

In a tiny room, the four babies lay motionless on bare army cots with no side rails. In their shaved heads were IV needles delivering badly needed fluids to their dehydrated bodies. Beside them, glass bottles hung from metal IV poles. Plastic accordion tubing from an aging humidifier sprayed a fine mist into their faces to help them breathe.

Rebecca brushed away the black flies on her daughter's glistening, spotted face. Laura was bathed in sweat and struggling to breathe. With no air conditioning, the cramped room was stifling.

Rebecca stepped into the bathroom. Flies swarmed over the toilet — a dirty hole in the ground. Over the doorknob was a dirty white gauze cover.

"She's not going to make it out of this hospital," Rebecca said quietly to her husband when she came back into the girls' room. "They're already so sick. In these Third-World conditions, they'll catch something else."

There was no medication to ease the babies' wheezing or reduce their fevers. No chest X-rays were available to help manage their treatment. The Blanks tried to feed Laura some Pedialyte that they'd brought from home. But when they tried to give her Tylenol, again they were stopped and reprimanded.

"But our babies have raging temperatures," Leslie Ponrick protested. "We have to cool them down."

Mr. Gu and Ken had tried hard to convince the hospital staff to use fever reducers, but their pleas were repeatedly overruled. The men knew the hospital staff were doing what they believed was best. Sharing their frustration, the pair tried to comfort the parents.

Aside from being present and offering their love, it seemed there was nothing the parents could do to help the babies. But the Blanks steadfastly refused to lose faith. "We trust in God for the lives of these babies," a weary David Blank said into the video camera as his wife recorded.

～

Lily stepped out of the airport into a flood of bicycles, buses, cars, and cabs on the jammed streets of Changsha. Mr. Gu was there to meet her with the latest update. The babies were in critical condition at the hospital. "Before you go," he said, "you must call your mother."

"She'll have to wait," Lily said, wanting to get to the families and their daughters as quickly as she could. But out of respect for the woman he'd known since he was a boy, Mr. Gu insisted. Lily knew it would be quicker to call than to argue, so she gave in.

"I know you love those babies, but you must take care of yourself," her mother warned Lily. "You're thirty-three years old, and you have never had the measles. Not many adults who get the measles survive."

"I have to do my job, Mama," she said steadily. "I have no choice. I can't leave these parents helpless with sick babies."

When Lily finally stepped into the crowded hospital room, the parents were huddled over their sick children who lay listless on the bare wooden cots in the oppressive heat. When they saw her face, they could not believe she was actually there. They had wondered if the head of CCAI would really fly all this way to their rescue.

Tom Ponrick felt his helpless sense of isolation lift at the sight of Lily.

Thank God. No matter what happens now, she'll be here to help us.

Several of the babies had been placed on oxygen. But oxygen alone was not enough for the Ponrick baby, who could no longer breathe on her own. A ventilator was breathing for Liu Fan.

In hushed tones, Lily pulled David Blank aside and consulted with him. He quickly gave her his assessment, hoping that now there might be some action. He was trying to remain calm, even though he'd been effectively relegated to the sidelines as the girls failed.

"They must be moved to intensive care — immediately," he told her.

Promising to get help, Lily strode from the room into the chaos of the hospital hallway. Her eyes searched the hall that was crowded with sick children and anxious parents. Nowhere could she see a doctor or nurse. Hurrying past the beds lined along the walls, she finally spotted a hospital worker. Lily knew she didn't have a minute to waste.

"Where is the president's office?" she demanded.

Silently, the woman pointed to another building. Lily hurried across the courtyard, bristling. On the flight to Changsha she'd prayed that the babies would hold on until she could get there. Now that she'd seen them, she concentrated only on how she would fight to keep them alive.

Pausing to gather herself, Lily walked into the president's office as if it were her own. She had no fear of the government official she would face; her only fear was that these children might die.

Erect and dignified, she handed over her business card with her name and title in both English and Chinese.

"I am here to complete the international adoption of four babies with measles," she said, her eyes boring into the woman's face. "Their parents have return tickets to America in just a few days."

Lily paused, emphasizing the enormity of what she was about to say.

"If their daughters die in your hospital, it will become an international event. The whole world will know."

The president blanched. Lily knew she had been heard.

The president quickly dialed the number of Dr. Liu Xiang Guo, director of the infectious disease department. When she hung up, she turned to Lily, her face tight, explaining the hospital would organize an emergency treatment committee. A doctor would be with the babies twenty-four hours a day.

"We will do everything we can for these children," she said. "But we cannot guarantee anything."

Soon Dr. Liu arrived, his face filled with kindness and concern. "The babies," he told Lily in broken English, "will be transferred to intensive care."

"Have you had the measles?" he asked.

"No — and my mom was quick to remind me. Is there anything I can do?"

"I'll give you a prescription for a shot to boost your immune system. If you're lucky, it might protect you."

Back in the pediatric ward, Lily announced to the parents that the babies were going to the intensive care unit. Her effort had moved the babies to the head of the class, but there was a downside: No visitors were allowed in the ICU. Their parents could no longer stay at their sides.

All they could do now was perch on an open, outdoor walkway — practically a ledge — and watch through the open fifth-floor windows as their sick daughters battled for their lives.

From their post in the blazing sun, the Blanks could see that conditions in the ICU were closer to those in Western pediatric units. Each baby had her own bed with side rails and clean sheets, and all finally received medication to reduce their fevers, although on a limited basis. The couple knew that more controlled conditions would greatly diminish the chance of infection spreading.

Still the lethargic babies were suffering from the sultry summer heat. Through the screenless windows came black flies that landed on their lips. Making things worse were the sickly smells hiding unsuccessfully amid swirls of smoke from burning incense that floated from the ICU. Lighting a match in a U.S. hospital in a room with oxygen tanks was strictly forbidden. Here, nurses lit incense in pots on the floor next to oxygen tanks in an ancient spiritual rite intended to cleanse the air.

Nevertheless, in this mysterious place where Western medicine met Eastern, the Blanks were encouraged. But Tom and Leslie Ponrick felt entirely hopeless.

Liu Fan seemed to be unconscious, breathing on the ventilator and nourished only by a feeding tube. They left her late that afternoon not knowing if she would make it through the night.

The next morning when the Americans returned to their post, they were surprised to find bits of shattered glass littering their ledge outside the ICU. From behind the now-closed windows came the steady hum of two air conditioners.

The parents stared at Lily in surprise but said nothing about the mysterious appearance of air conditioners. When Dr. Liu questioned her, Lily quietly explained that the units were a donation from Chinese Children Adoption International.

Side by side, Lily and Ken stood with the parents in the melting heat, watching, pacing, and waiting for the next update on the babies. Ever since Lily's arrival, she had been hungry. With no time for meals, she survived on energy bars and water. "You have to eat," Ken said, encouraging her to go find real food. But she refused and insisted on staying. She feared that as soon as she stepped away, she would miss a new report on the babies.

When they came, the updates from Dr. Liu were encouraging — except for the Ponrick baby.

With a slow, eerie rhythm, the life-support machine breathed in and out for the child. Its unnatural groaning sounds grated on Lily's ears. Because even the slightest motion would impede the ventilator's effectiveness, doctors had given Liu Fan medication to temporarily paralyze her and keep her from fighting the machine.

As Lily stood on the outdoor ledge looking in, her heart ached.

This baby belongs to us, and here we are watching her die on that bed.

Lily was doing everything in her power to try to hasten the recovery of the babies. The deadline for their departure was fast approaching. If the babies weren't released in time to fly to Guangzhou, they would miss their long-scheduled appointment with the U.S. Consulate to get their visas. Without the visas, the children could not leave China.

To the Blanks, the whole situation was bewildering. Even if the babies were released in time to make the flight, the couple wondered if the U.S. Consulate would believe these measles-scabbed babies were not contagious. Lily was doing what she could to convince the medical officials to let the babies go, but she confided in the Blanks that it might not be enough. And changing international flights for the more than thirty parents and babies in their group would be next to impossible.

In a private moment with Rebecca and David, as they wrestled with what to do, Lily shared the motto she now lived by, "Pray. Do my part, and leave the rest to God."

If the babies didn't get better, the Blanks wondered, what would come next? They were aware that the orphanage would let them adopt another child if that's what they wanted. But from the beginning of the adoption process, it was their belief that God had chosen this child for them. When they received Laura's match picture, they knew she was the child they had prayed for. Now, in this critical moment of uncertainty, they could not even bear to think of leaving without their daughter.

Back at the hotel, Tom and Leslie Ponrick had no choice but to face that heart-wrenching decision. When Lily knocked on the door of their room, the couple knew why she had come. Delivering the doctor's devastating prognosis was the hardest thing she'd ever done as the leader of CCAI. In Lily's sad eyes, the couple saw the compassion of a mother who shared their heartbreak. Gently, she confirmed what they had dreaded hearing. Liu Fan was not going to get better.

Tom Ponrick was crushed by the wave of emotion, and Leslie struggled not to break down. They had witnessed Liu Fan's struggle for survival, but her body was not strong enough for the fight. Now they would be going home without the daughter they had come so far to get. Grief flooded the room as they realized they would never see Liu Fan again.

Slowly, Lily began to share with them the phone call she made that morning to the orphanage. The officials wanted the Ponricks to know that another baby girl was waiting for them if they wanted her.

Leslie knew the answer. Tears trailing down her face, she told her husband, "I am not leaving China without a baby."

Her nickname was Ya Bao, and she was just three months old.

A caretaker at the orphanage placed the baby in Lily's arms while Tom taped the arrival of the child who would now be their daughter.

"Here's your new baby, your little girl," Lily said, her voice filled with encouragement. Lovingly, she put the child into the quivering arms of her mother.

"Olivia Mariah finally joins our family," Tom announced.

Cradling her baby, Leslie looked down into the child's sweet face, calling out softly, "Little Grasshopper." It was the nickname from the Kung Fu films of the seventies that Tom had given their daughter months before she entered their life.

As she kissed her baby's forehead, the aching sadness in Leslie's heart was slowly mixed with joy. She was sure that this baby was meant to be hers.

It would be ten years later that Olivia Ponrick would write on the white board in their kitchen the words that her mother would never forget:

The things we lose have a way of coming back to us, just not in the way we expected.

On the day Lily worried would never come, she stood outside on the fifth-floor ledge, beaming. Wearing a T-shirt that said, "Born in China, Loved in the U.S.," she watched a nurse hand little Laura Blank out the ICU door directly into her mother's arms. The IV had been pulled from the baby's shaved head, and she wore the new dress her mother had bought her.

At last Rebecca Blank was able to let the tears flow freely. At her side, her husband choked back his emotions as the babies he'd tried so hard to help were delivered to their elated parents.

For the first time since her emergency arrival, Lily basked in the happiness on the back side of the suffering and loss she'd seen. All eleven families would go home with baby girls. Lily invited the families and the children to a celebration feast at the hotel to mark the end of the long ordeal in Changsha.

As she rose from the table to speak, she seemed a changed woman. Their serious, strong leader was radiant. With the home video cameras rolling, she thanked God for their babies.

"This is a group with a lot of emotional struggles and a lot of emotional support," she told the families. "You definitely made CCAI history. Congratulations to the nervous parents and strong parents."

Then she introduced Dr. Liu. "He's the one who saved our babies' lives."

And she's the saint, thought Tom Ponrick, *who rescued us all.*

One last hurdle stood ahead of them in Guangzhou. Lily had arranged for Raymond, her trusted representative in Guangdong's capital city, to meet the families and navigate the final critical checkpoints that would free them to leave China with their children.

The scabs on the babies were healing, but Lily worried they might impede their journey home. The doctors performing the necessary physical exams would not sign the required papers if they thought the babies might still be contagious. And the U.S. Consulate would not issue visas to any babies considered infected.

On Sunday before their departure from Changsha, Lily and several families took their worries to one of the city's few Christian churches. As they arrived to worship, from the windows they heard the sweet notes of "Amazing Grace."

"Peace be with you," a Chinese greeter called out in English, welcoming the Americans. In a section reserved for foreigners, they listened to the sermon in Mandarin. David Blank videotaped, quietly recording his own words, "God is good."

At the airport that afternoon, the families would at last fly to Guangzhou, while Lily headed to Hong Kong to meet Art and Amy, who were flying thousands of miles without her.

One by one the adoptive parents embraced her, their eyes brimming with tears and hearts overflowing with thankfulness for the woman who had rescued their babies. *Without her,* Tom Ponrick wondered, *would the babies ever have gotten the care they so desperately needed? Would I be leaving China with this baby in my arms?*

At the medical center in Guangzhou, Raymond steered the families in Group Thirty-One through the maze of medical examinations. Nervously, they searched the face of the doctor to see how he reacted to the crusty scabs on their babies' faces. To their amazement, the doctor made no comment.

After they made it through, Raymond remained behind to finish the paperwork. The families had one final mission: the U.S. Consulate. Shortly before their visa appointment, babies in tow, they gathered in front of the

White Swan Hotel to walk to the consulate building next door.

"Where's Raymond?" someone asked.

Nobody knew, and the clock was ticking. Frantic, the families stationed lookouts up and down the street to watch for him. Time was running out. If they didn't go now, they would miss their appointment. As they turned to leave, Raymond at last came running up the street, sweat streaming down his face. With no time for explanations, he hustled the parade of families to the consulate.

Never were the Americans so grateful to see the United States flag flying high in the sky. Less than an hour later, Group Thirty-One walked out of the U.S. Consulate, carrying their babies and their visas. What kept Raymond at the medical center they would never know. The families were too tired and relieved to care.

Finally, they were going home.

Maybe this one will be different.

TWELVE

VISION OF HOPE
1996

Yet another wave of weary passengers filed out of the customs gate in the Hong Kong airport, and Lily's anxious eyes scoured the crowd in search of Art and Amy. She wondered if these stern officials would even allow six-year-olds out of customs without their parents.

The twins had been in the air for nearly fifteen hours with a couple from Group Thirty-Four who had agreed to watch over them. Both children had asthma, and the poor air circulation on long flights often made it hard for them to breathe. Lily closed her eyes and took a deep breath, trying to calm her racing heart. When she looked up, Art and Amy were running to her, excitement on their faces.

Not once in the time she had spent watching over the babies with measles had Lily allowed herself to cry. A strong, clear mind had been essential. But now, with the twins at last in her grasp, she let the pent-up tears go.

Before they boarded yet another plane to Nanning, she dialed home to let Joshua know that their children were safe. Their brief conversation was cordial, but restrained. As she hung up, she knew that her husband's move back home was only the first tentative step. Their journey toward reconciliation would take time.

Lily focused her thoughts on Group Thirty-Four's next stop in Nanning in the southwestern province of Guangxi. The families would receive eight babies from Guilin, the town where her mother grew up, and three from an orphanage in Nanning known as Mother's Love. The first time she heard the name, Lily felt a fleeting hope.

Maybe this one will be different.

Settling her children into the seats beside her, she said a silent prayer of thanksgiving for their uneventful flight from America, followed by an urgent plea.

Please don't let me have measles.

The twins weren't at risk; both had been vaccinated. But if she were infected, Lily could give the measles to the babies who were about to be united with their families. With no local CCAI representative in Guangxi, she had no choice but to take the risk.

"Be ready," she warned in a phone call to Mr. Gu, who was leading a group of families in another province. "If I get sick, you'll have to come."

Her apprehension heightened that night when the nannies arrived at the hotel in Nanning with seven babies worn out after a grueling eight-hour train ride from Guilin. The babies were thin and frail, and their tiny socks slouched around ankles that seemed only slightly bigger than Lily's thumb. Unable for months to move their arms or legs under the layers of clothing they had worn, the weak babies felt like undersized sacks of rice in their parents' arms. One toddler's crouched legs refused to hang straight. Lily had seen those bowed legs before on babies who had been left for hours on wooden potty chairs before they were even strong enough to sit.

She peered into the babies' pale faces. They were blank, seemingly resigned to a fate over which they had no control. Seeing their bony bodies, Lily felt a familiar anger slowly rise inside her. In the past year, she had visited more than a dozen rundown orphanages across China, but never had she seen a group of babies so severely malnourished as this one from Guilin.

It had been twenty years since she visited her grandmother's hometown, a two-thousand-year-old city called the Bright Pearl of China. But she vividly remembered the natural grandeur of the city on the crystal clear Li River encircled by its strangely shaped green peaks. A famous poem said it best:

Shui shi lu yin dai, shan ru bi yu zhan.
The river is a green silk ribbon, the hills are jade hair pins.

Lily could not fathom what kind of dark place in that thriving tourist mecca cared so little for its babies that they barely bothered to feed them. She knew with frequent feedings and the tender care of their new parents that these fragile babies would soon grow strong, but that knowledge could not hold back the tide of her dismay.

The following morning, Lily climbed into a bus with Art and Amy and three families who would get their daughters that day. It was the second adoption trip to China for David and Janet Schroeder, who were in the first group that Lily led to China in 1995. The young couple from Colorado thought they knew what to expect after getting their first baby, Emily, in Kunming. But after seeing the fragile babies from Guilin, they realized that they had no idea what they would find when they were united with their second child, Katherine.

Leaving the noisy heart of Nanning behind, the bus rambled into the peace and quiet of the city's verdant outskirts. Soon, they were climbing a long narrow road up a hill and pulling up to a huge, white stone building.

Many of China's buildings seemed dingy and rundown even after just a few years of use. But this building was so clean it practically gleamed. In the courtyard connecting the two wings was a six-sided pagoda with a red tile roof sweeping gracefully into the sky. Lily stopped to take in the unexpected sight.

This is an orphanage?

In the tidy courtyard, the green grass was neatly trimmed. Gracing the entrance was a life-sized, white stone figure of a reclining woman reaching out to a small child. The name of the statue was Mother's Love.

Inside the building, the walls were painted bright white and the floors polished to a shine. The scent of fresh soap filled the air. Lily could not believe her nose — or her eyes.

The forbidding cold and darkness she'd seen in so many orphanages was replaced here by rays of sunlight, streaming through the floor-to-ceiling windows. Outside it was sticky hot, but inside, ceiling fans kept the rooms cool and comfortable.

A pretty, young woman wearing a simple silver cross introduced herself — in English — as Kit Ying Chan. Never before had Lily heard a Chinese orphanage official speak English. Kit Ying explained that she was born and raised in Hong Kong. Her soft voice thanked the Americans who had come all this way to give homes to the children of Mother's Love.

Hearing the soothing sound of Kit Ying's words brought a flood of images to Lily. Too often she had seen brusque orphanage officials treat children like merchandise instead of human beings. In this woman's spirit, Lily could see her passion for abandoned children.

The idea at Mother's Love, Kit Ying explained, is to provide each child with the best individualized care available. The goal was to nurture children back to health within a few months of their abandonment so they could be temporarily placed into loving homes of local Chinese residents trained in foster care. On this day, fifty-three babies were at Mother's Love, but an additional 156 children were living in foster homes.

Turning to the families, Kit Ying gave a gentle warning. "It may take time for the babies to grieve the loss of their foster parents," she said, "and adjust to their new families." Janet Schroeder heard the director's words, but still she was not prepared for what she was about to experience.

The listless babies from Guilin had been silent when placed into the arms of their new parents. But Katherine Schroeder, who at twenty months weighed no more than a one-year-old, came to her new mother whimpering. Janet quietly tried to comfort the toddler, but Katherine's cries only grew louder.

Waiting outside the room was the older daughter from the foster family who had cared for the girl they knew as Xiao Zhu for more than a year. Kit Ying asked the Schroeders for permission to allow the young woman in her early twenties to say goodbye. Janet looked at her husband, then nodded yes.

Still whimpering as she clutched a stuffed animal, Katherine wailed so hard when she saw her foster sister that her stubby pigtails shook. The young woman took the girl into her arms one last time, and Katherine clung to her. Tears spilled down the young woman's face, and Janet Schroeder felt her own eyes brimming as she wrapped her arms around both of them and kissed her daughter's foster sister on the cheek. When the young woman from the only family Katherine knew started to leave, the girl sobbed until she spit up.

The love between this child and her foster sister was unlike any Lily had ever witnessed in China's orphanages. She stared at Kit Ying in awe.

Janet was still trying to console her daughter when Kit Ying amazed Lily again. The director handed the Schroeders an unexpected treasure — photographs documenting the beginnings of their baby's life, along with written reports describing her personality, development, diet, sleep patterns, and likes and dislikes. From Katherine's foster family, the Schroeders received two notes, along with the girl's favorite red-and-white ball.

Soon it was time for the families to leave with their daughters, but Lily was determined to see more of Mother's Love.

From the door of the nursery, Lily heard a noise she'd never heard inside the walls of an orphanage: joy. The huge room was lined with cribs, but all of them were empty. It was playtime at Mother's Love.

On a brightly colored mat dotted with toys, caretakers laughed and played on the floor with the babies. Cooing to the children, they looked into their eyes, calling them by English names they had been given. Freshly bathed, the sweet-smelling babies wore clean, new clothes.

Lily felt as if she were walking through some wondrous dream.

Until then, she had known two types of institutionalized children. One was completely shut down, with no emotion in her face, only the numbness of a child who had given up. Early on, this child had learned that crying got her nothing. The other type was aggressive, wailing and fussy, with the fierceness of a fighter. This child clung furiously to the false conviction that if she kept screaming someone would come. No matter what the type, the babies were delayed, both developmentally and emotionally.

At Mother's Love, Lily was discovering another kind of baby, a child safe and content enough to explore the world around her and to freely express her budding personality. In this peaceful place, Lily felt the presence of love.

"You're so young and you're from Hong Kong," Lily said, incredulous. "How could you make this happen in China?"

Kit Ying led Lily and the twins into the milk room as she shared the story of the birth of Mother's Love.

A social worker for Mother's Choice orphanage in Hong Kong, Kit Ying was in her twenties when she heard about the dire conditions in an orphanage in Nanning. She decided to see for herself and found malnourished babies packed four and five to each rusty crib. One sick baby caught her eye and tugged at her heart, and she spent the afternoon holding her.

Emboldened, she convinced the director to allow her to take the girl back to her hotel room for the night. She fed her and treated the baby's bloody sores from diarrhea. The next morning, she couldn't bear to bring the child back. Friends at Mother's Choice helped her find a family for the child, and later that year she found homes for more Nanning orphans. China was open to finding ways to improve its orphanage care, and within a few years the Guangxi Department of Civil Affairs agreed to partner with Mother's Choice to open Mother's Love in a building that once housed retired officials. Frightened at first by the idea of overseeing such a huge child-care operation, Kit Ying decided to use a child-centered management system to provide individualized care for each baby.

In the milk room, Kit Ying opened the refrigerator to show Lily how feeding time worked. Inside were rows of bottles, each with a baby's name on it. No bottles were shared as they were in other orphanages, where bottle-swapping quickly spread disease. On the wall were feeding instructions for each baby with the amount of formula based on a child's weight, age, and health.

As they walked into the washing room, Lily could see that every piece of clothing was labeled with a child's name. A worker was neatly folding and stacking the clothes that in the other institutions she had visited were heaped into a jumbled pile and rifled through by caretakers in search of anything that might fit.

Lily glanced at Kit Ying, shaking her head in astonishment. In the Chinese institutional care she'd known, there was no room for individualism.

"Let me show you one more thing," the director told Lily, gently taking her arm.

She opened a door into the backyard. There staked in the grass in front of a red brick wall was a neat row of small, white crosses. Without a word from Kit Ying, Lily understood. These were the graves of the abandoned babies whom Mother's Love had been unable to save. Thousands of other children had died in China's orphanages. But before this day, before this place, Lily had never seen a tribute to the short lives of abandoned children whose graves would never be visited by their parents. Lily could feel her eyes filling as her heart wept.

What she had seen at Mother's Love was beyond anything she could have imagined. Turning to Kit Ying to say goodbye, instead of the formal handshake that was customary, Lily embraced the director like a sister.

The twins asleep in the bed next to her, Lily lay wide awake, thinking back to all she'd seen since bringing her first group of families to China. By the end of 1995, she was overwhelmed by the urgent need to keep abandoned children alive by trying to feed them. Joshua had raised thousands of dollars, knowing that each day, each meal was crucial to the children's survival.

In 1996, she had recognized an entirely different need. At a reunion for the families in Group One, she listened to the Chinese toddlers speaking English and instantly felt an imperative to teach CCAI's adopted children their native Mandarin. Joshua helped his wife launch a Chinese cultural school for adopted children, the Joyous Chinese Cultural Center.

Now after touring Mother's Love, Lily could see there was so much more that she and her husband could do. At home, they were taking their first steps toward mending their broken marriage. The process of healing the hurt and restoring trust could not be hurried. But the Chinese children they felt summoned to help could not wait.

By year's end, CCAI would bring home more than four hundred babies. The couple began to envision placing not hundreds, but thousands by expanding the agency beyond the borders of Colorado to get children out of China and into families faster.

Mother's Love had shown Lily yet another way they could make a fundamental difference in the lives of abandoned children.

She called Colorado. She knew Joshua was counting the days until his family's return home, but she could think only of sharing with him the miracle she had just witnessed. Talking with Joshua, Lily gave him a blow-by-blow account of Mother's Love, painting images colored by details of light and joy.

"I wonder what it would take to turn an orphanage into a Mother's Love?" she asked.

"I don't know, but I'll find out."

Later that year, he flew to China to see Mother's Love for himself. Joshua was overwhelmed, and he returned home convinced that opening an orphanage was something they could do.

He took her by surprise when he told his wife, "We'll name it Lily Orphan Care Center."

Before they were able to make that dream a reality, four years would pass, and CCAI would bring more than two thousand babies from 146 orphanages in sixteen Chinese provinces to loving families.

This job is not just to make a living.
It's about saving and changing children's lives.

THIRTEEN

PLANTING SEEDS
2000

At the turn of the twenty-first century, China announced to the world a new liberalized policy allowing joint ventures with foreigners. It was the opening Lily and Joshua had been waiting for. Nearly a decade had passed since their homeland had opened its doors to adoption, and the Chinese were making some strides in improving orphanage care. When Joshua approached the Ministry of Civil Affairs in the province of Zhejiang, the director quickly agreed to allow Chinese Children Adoption International to open the first model Lily Orphan Care Center at the orphanage in Hangzhou, the beautiful West Lake city whose official flower was *Bai He Hua,* the lily.

It had been five years since Lily had first visited the orphanage. From the outside, the building still appeared well-tended, with its neatly kept yard. But inside, thirty babies had reportedly died of dehydration from diarrhea that previous summer.

Lily understood how fast bacteria could sweep through an understaffed orphanage. For hours babies lay in dirty diapers, waiting for a caretaker who never seemed to come while rashes and open sores festered. Soiled diapers were heaped in reeking piles in the corners of the room until they were collected for washing. For days, babies lay in cribs in the same set of clothes. It was only when a leaky diaper soiled a baby's leggings or shirt that the clothing was changed. At feeding time, if a baby failed to finish her formula, the used bottle was propped into another hungry mouth.

In most of southeastern China, orphanages had no heat or hot water, and babies received no baths during winter. In Hangzhou, children were occasionally dunked in a single tub of lukewarm water, one after the other. When the bath turned a murky gray with the dirt of several children, the filthy water was finally changed.

At night, there was sometimes one caretaker for scores of children, and by early morning the orphanage was screaming with the cries of hungry babies who hadn't been fed since the evening before. Some of the orphanage's two-year-olds still drank bottles of *congee,* a thin rice porridge. They had no idea how to eat solid food.

Heads shaved and clothes mismatched, girls could not be told from boys. The abandoned children were all given the same surname at the orphanage, but rarely did they hear the sound of the Chinese first names they were assigned.

No doctor or nurse came to tend the sick, and there was no medication to treat illness. Even the gravely ill were not taken to the hospital, an hour's drive away. In the worst cases, sick children paid with their lives.

The first time Lily entered the Hangzhou orphanage in 1995, it seemed almost too much to bear. Now, five years later Joshua had worked feverishly to raise the hundred thousand dollars needed to transform this grim place into a model orphan care center.

Remodeling the rundown building in Hangzhou and changing the deeply ingrained culture of the orphanage would require a revolution, and Lily and Joshua persuaded his younger sister to lead it.

Xia Zhong was the one who had pleaded with her brother years before to stop wasting time pursuing that Nie girl. But over time, the two women had grown to love and respect each other. Tough and smart, Xia had the heart and the will to make the drastic change that was required.

She had moved from China to Colorado to live with her brother's family while she worked and learned English. In the year 2000, at the age of thirty-six, she was the oldest student at Spring International Language Institute, the school where Lily had learned to speak English a dozen years earlier.

A mother, Xia had raised one son, but she knew nothing about running a massive child-care operation. Lily sent her to Nanning to learn from the experts, Kit Ying and the child-care professionals at Mother's Love. From Kit Ying, Xia learned the systematic method of individualized child care: how to set up a proper milk kitchen, infant care room, and nursery. Xia then flew to Hangzhou to undertake the extensive remodeling of the building that would become Lily Orphan Care Center. But she soon found that her most daunting challenge had nothing to do with construction.

As she worked alongside the caretakers, Xia could see that some did not care about the lives of the children who depended on them. They made it clear:

This is not my baby. This is not my home. There's more than enough work to do, feeding and changing dozens of babies each day. Holding babies is not my job.

In China, work as an orphanage caretaker was considered little better than a job as a trash collector. The conditions were cold, dirty, and smelly, the hours long and exhausting, the work backbreaking, and the pay barely enough to feed a family.

Overthrowing the old orphanage culture would require firing, hiring, training, and reorganizing. But Lily knew what would come hardest for the nannies would be a change of heart. For the children to truly flourish, the caretakers must love and care for these babies as if they were their own.

In the many phone calls between Denver and Hangzhou, Lily coached her sister-in-law. "Tell them everyone needs a job," she said, "but this job is not just to make a living. It's about saving and changing children's lives."

She asked Xia to show them how to do it by becoming the "Big Mom."

Xia started with one tiny girl, just two years old. The child's thin body was covered with the ugly scars of abuse suffered before she was abandoned. Her worst wounds, though, were invisible. The girl refused to speak or even look at anyone. The caretakers simply ignored her.

At first when Xia tried to approach her, the child turned away. Each day, the new orphanage director returned, speaking soothingly to her. One afternoon, Xia lay down on the floor beside her.

"I am here," she said in a comforting voice. "I am waiting for you."

For several days, the caretakers watched their boss's failed attempts to connect with the isolated girl. They shook their heads and grumbled, "Why does she waste the time?"

A week passed. One morning, when Xia arrived at the orphanage, the girl walked up to her and looked into her eyes. Xia smiled.

"Now, that's not so difficult," Xia said, gently touching the child's bony shoulder.

On the mornings that followed, Xia arrived at the orphanage with a small gift — a toy, a trinket, or a piece of candy, anything to make the girl feel special. When the director walked into the room, the child she had begun to love went to her, her sad face lighting up expectantly.

When the nannies saw what had happened, they began calling her "Big Mom's baby."

Each nanny was assigned her own six children, and soon all infants at Lily Orphan Care Center were being fed in the arms of a human being. At feeding time the entire staff, from the kitchen workers and housekeepers to the nurses and the new resident doctor, headed to the children's rooms to help. Every baby was hand-fed from an individually labeled bottle until it was empty, no matter how long it took. Shift leaders checked the bottles and monitored the refrigerators to make sure by day's end each child had received five full bottles. In the kitchen, four full-time workers shopped, sterilized bottles, and measured and mixed formula based on each baby's nutritional needs. They chopped and cooked vegetables and meat for the toddlers who no longer subsisted on bottles of congee.

Lily next asked Xia to do the unthinkable: Peel off the multiple layers of clothing that kept the babies in bondage. With heat now installed in the Lily Orphan Care Center, Xia told the nannies that babies no longer needed many layers for warmth. Under Xia's watchful eyes, the nannies obediently removed the babies' extra clothing. But when the Big Mom left the room, they quickly put the layers back on. Xia was exasperated, but Lily encouraged her not to give up. Patiently, Xia pointed out to the nannies the monitors in each room showing the temperature was a warm sixty-five degrees. "See," she said. "The babies can wear only a sweater and be comfortable."

No matter what Xia said, it was a losing battle. In the end, she was not the deciding factor. The kids were. What finally convinced the caretakers was the delight on the children's faces when they were freed to move and discover the existence of their own hands and feet.

With bath time now daily in a fresh sink of water, the babies freely splashed and played. The nannies took their time with the bath, singing songs and chattering to each child as they scrubbed.

"First, let's wash your ears; they're for hearing," the nannies chirped. "Now, let's clean your eyes; they're for seeing."

It was unmistakable. New life was awakening at Lily Orphan Care Center. One morning there was new pastel cloth printed with red hearts to make nanny uniforms. Next came mobiles to put over the babies' cribs, toys for them to chew on, and animal and flower pictures to decorate their rooms.

In their faces and their voices, Xia could see the nannies becoming attached to their children.

"Look at my baby," one nanny beamed, holding up a small girl to Xia. "She's doing very well."

Like little flowers given some water, the children — and their nannies — were beginning to bloom.

You are here for a reason.

FOURTEEN

LIKE FAMILY
2001

In the heat of the summer, Lily and Joshua returned to China together for the first time since leaving their homeland fifteen years earlier. She was nearly thirty-eight; he was thirty-nine. Through hard work, patience, and faith, the couple had found their way back to each other, strengthened by a renewed love. As a family, with Amy and Art, now eleven, they walked through the doorway of the first Lily Orphan Care Center.

Xia gathered her niece and nephew into her arms, her eyes shining. Unable to contain her excitement, she hurried her brother's family down the hall to the nursery.

The walls were sky blue and sunny yellow, and the soothing sounds of classical music and children's melodies filled the air. On a huge carpeted area, dozens of children played, their bright eyes fully alive, their chubby cheeks flushed pink. The shiny black hair on many girls had grown long enough to tell them apart from the few boys.

On the floor with the babies sat their nannies, dressed in uniforms of soft pastels. Climbing in and out of their caretakers' laps, the children crawled across the carpet to grab new toys. On one side of the room, toddlers sped down a miniature slide, squealing in glee. On the other, a young girl rocked back and forth on a large toy horse.

Lily lowered herself to the floor and pulled a crawling baby into her lap. She held the sweet-smelling girl to her chest, then lifted her high into the air, bouncing the laughing baby up and down. Soon the twins were on all fours crawling through the maze of children, waving toys before their curious faces.

Lily followed Xia into the milk room. Sterilized bottles were labeled with babies' names, and feeding schedules were posted on the wall. In the bath room were sinks for daily bathing and stacks of fresh towels. In the wash room, freshly laundered clothes were neatly folded and labeled with each child's name.

"It's another Mother's Love," Lily said, exuberant. "But even better!"

Lily Orphan Care Center would be a model for delivering first-class care to abandoned children, and it would serve as a training ground for thousands of caretakers coming from orphanages across China.

"I don't know if you noticed before, but we have one thing here that you won't find at any orphanage," Xia said. "Follow me."

Back in the nursery, across one wall, was a long mirror. Lily watched a toddler pull herself up to stand, placing both tiny hands flat on the mirror. Staring, the girl giggled and touched the reflection of her small face. She had come to this orphanage alone in the world with no name. Now, this confident girl had a new name and would soon have a new family.

"*Hao bao bao,*" Lily whispered, sitting down next to the mirror.

The girl's nanny laughed with the child. Then she swooped the girl into her arms, bathing her forehead with kisses.

"Like family," Lily said her luminous eyes locking with Joshua's.

He sat down next to his wife. It had been nearly a decade since they'd started the journey that led them into the human hell of China's orphanages, divided their own hearts, and bound them back together. Now, in this moment, they were enveloped in a small piece of heaven. The Lily Orphan Care Center was still an institution, but it was a place where those once rejected would be given a second chance to find the love they'd lost.

Turning back to the child with the rosy cheeks playing before her, a shadow swept over Lily's heart. She knew, deep down, that one day the little girl in the mirror would wrestle with the pain of having been abandoned.

To the adopted Chinese children who would come to her looking for answers, Lily knew she would offer the same invitation she had once accepted. An invitation to choose the peace that comes with the healing grace found through forgiveness.

Your birth parents made a choice under certain conditions. You must trust that there's a reason they made it. Try not to punish yourself because of their choice. Try to find a way to forgive them. Whether it was right or wrong, it is hard to know. My mom chose to keep me, and if you look at my life, I believe there's a reason.

Look at your life.

You are here for a reason.

EPILOGUE
2009

The story of Lily Nie, Joshua Zhong, and Chinese Children Adoption International is by no means over, and many would say that it will continue for generations, bound up in the stories of thousands of adoptive families. In partnership with China, Lily, Joshua, and their dedicated staff of more than one hundred in the U.S. and China had, by the end of 2009, united 8,638 abandoned children with families in sixteen countries. All but about six hundred are girls. Half of CCAI's families have returned to China to adopt a second child, one-fifth went back for a third adoption, and one percent have adopted four or more Chinese children.

More than eighty thousand adopted Chinese children now live in the U.S. At the height of Chinese adoption in 2005, CCAI was placing kids at a pace of more than four children per business day. By the end of 2009, the economic and political climate in China had dropped that number to about three children every two business days. Despite the slowdown, CCAI remains the world's largest China-focused adoption agency.

In the seventeen years since the founding of CCAI, Lily, Joshua, and the CCAI staff have built it into far more than a traditional adoption agency. CCAI continues to strive to help abandoned children left behind in China by meeting basic food, clothing, and other needs; providing training for nannies and foster care for orphans; and offering medical and educational support and disaster relief. At home, the agency attempts to meet the changing needs of CCAI's adopted children.

"We brought these Chinese children to this country, and we're responsible for making their lives better," Lily said. "Whatever their need, we try to meet it."

In 2004, Lily and Joshua got to experience the process from a whole new perspective, following in the footsteps of their adoptive families. They brought into their family a nine-year-old girl whose severe heart condition once branded her unadoptable. Hua Gao Jie became Anna Jie Zhong.

Lily and Joshua strive to help CCAI's children see their potential and use their talents to one day influence the world.

"You have potential that you don't know you have," Lily tells adoptees. "When I grew up, I never knew I could do all the things that I have done."

Chinese Children Charity Fund

In Guizhou, one of China's poorest provinces, orphanage children wearing one thin layer of clothing walked twenty minutes to school in below-freezing temperatures. Other school-age girls and boys slept in toddler beds so small the children fell out. Still others with no meat or fish to eat could not get enough protein to maintain healthy growth. The Chinese Children Charity Fund team based in China brought them warm clothes, bicycles, beds, and fresh milk.

— Chinese Children Charity Fund Report, 2006

That first year, when Lily flew nine times to China and descended into forty orphanages, she was overwhelmed by the malnourishment suffered by many orphanage children. She and Joshua started with the mission of finding homes for abandoned children, but what they found in some of their homeland's orphanages were babies fighting for their lives. In the mid-1990s, one out of three orphanage infants reportedly died before reaching six months. Lily knew that before these babies could be adopted they must be fed.

CCAI expanded its mission in 1995 by founding the Chinese Orphan Formula Fund, and Joshua raised four thousand dollars to send emergency infant formula to orphanage children in Beijing and Hebei Province. Over the next year, Lily witnessed the dire need for more than just food. She found sick babies in dirty clothing with no medicine in orphanages with no heat or hot water. In 1996, the formula fund expanded to become the Chinese Children Charity Fund.

Over the years, the charity's four million dollars in contributions have helped provide orphanage children with heat in the winter, air-conditioning in the summer, medical care, and more. Adoptive families help fund those basic needs, along with washing machines, dryers, toys, microwaves, bottle-sterilization machines, cribs, walkers, and wheelchairs to improve the quality of life for those left behind. In partnership with the "Blankets for Babies" project begun by adoptive mother Karen Bradley, the charity fund also has helped deliver more than four thousand blankets to keep orphanage children warm.

Disaster relief is also provided by the charity fund, which sent seventy thousand dollars to rebuild orphanages in Hunan, Hubei, Jiangxi, and Fujian after the one-hundred-year flood in 1998 and more than one hundred and forty thousand dollars to rebuild orphanages after the 2008 Wenchuan, Sichuan, earthquake took the lives of about ninety thousand people.

More than half of China's orphanage children live with physical handicaps and little hope for adoption. The charity fund partners with doctors and charitable groups to establish on-site clinics, hire doctors and nurses, and donate medical equipment. Medical missions to China's orphanages enable children to receive surgeries to correct numerous physical defects. The Chinese Children Charity Fund pledged three hundred and fifty thousand dollars to Project Tomorrow for heart operations, cleft-lip, and cleft-palate surgeries for children in more than three hundred orphanages. CCAI's Three Mei's (little sisters) Therapy Program sends occupational and physical therapists to China to provide post-surgery rehabilitation to children after their procedures.

For children in orphanages that cannot afford the cost of school, CCAI's charity fund helps finance formal education, occupational-skills training, and even college education to give orphans a chance to earn a living when they reach eighteen and leave the only home many have ever known. The LOOK Project (Loving Older Orphanage Kids), spearheaded by a group of adoptive CCAI moms, partners with the charity fund to provide older children with health-care skills and knowledge they will need to function as independent, productive, healthy adults living on their own.

CCAI's charity fund team based in China travels to orphanages to identify the needs of abandoned children. In coordination with CCAI's network of loyal local representatives who see needs when they visit China's orphanages, the charity team provides food, clothes, furniture, appliances, and other basic essentials.

For more than a dozen years, the charity fund's efforts have improved the quality of life for thousands of orphanage children across China. In recognition of its humanitarian efforts, Chinese Children Charity Fund in 2007 became the first foreign charity to receive a Charity Certificate from the Chinese Ministry of Civil Affairs, allowing CCAI more access to the orphaned children of China who receive the least care.

Joyous Chinese Cultural Center

When five-year-old Malena returned to the Social Welfare Institute that made sure she was cared for in her first eleven months of life, she was greeted by her Chinese name. "Meng Han!" the staff called out. Moments later, she was walking hand in hand with the orphanage director to a conference room that had been prepared for her family's return visit. Malena beamed as the workers fussed over her — giving her a small gift, admiring her hair, and looking at pictures of her daily life in America that she had chosen to share with them. When she climbed onto the director's lap and said a few words in Mandarin, the staff's faces lit up. Moments later Malena quietly began to sing. The director leaned in and listened, a smile spreading across her face. It wasn't an American song; it was a traditional Chinese folk song, one that children all across China learned by heart. A song that Malena had learned at the Joyous Chinese Cultural Center.

— Jiangxi Province, 2006

It was at the first "Gotcha Day" anniversary party, celebrating the day Group One first held their adopted children, that Lily first heard China-born toddlers speaking English. She was awed by what she saw, but she also knew instantly that she must teach these Chinese children the language of their homeland.

"When I first came here, people treated me like a baby because I couldn't speak the language," Lily said. "I wanted to make sure these girls would know how to speak their native language."

Concerned about how CCAI's adopted children would be viewed if they spoke no Chinese, Lily wanted to do all she could to help build their confidence and self-esteem.

"When people asked where they were from, I wanted them to say with pride, 'China.' When people asked if they spoke and wrote Chinese, I wanted them to answer with confidence: 'Yes.'"

In 1996 after CCAI had brought thirty groups of adopted children home from China, the agency opened the Joyous Chinese Cultural Center with a dozen two- and three-year-old students. Lily started by teaching them simple Mandarin words: *ni hao* (hello), *zai jian* (goodbye), *xie xie* (thank you).

Victoria and Chris Lierheimer, adoptive parents and owners of a Colorado day-care center, soon volunteered to help with the school, turning it into a playful learning environment. When enrollment surged, Lily and Joshua hired educator Kat LaMons as the first paid director of the school.

"Lily and Josh are not experts in early childhood education, and I didn't know anything about Chinese culture," said Kat, who created the first formal curriculum. "I think it was God's little left turn for me."

The school hired teachers who had emigrated from mainland China, and the center became a place where adopted children got to be around Chinese adults and learned not only their native language but the arts, songs, dance, traditions, and foods of their birth country. The center also offers basic conversational Mandarin classes for adults and special adoption-travel language classes to assist parents adopting in China.

The cultural center grew to four hundred students at the Centennial, Colorado, campus and unexpectedly evolved into something Lily and Joshua hadn't envisioned. It became a gathering place for adopted Chinese children to be with families that looked like theirs and to start figuring out their own identity and origin. For adoptive parents, it became a support system to share their common adoption experience.

The cultural center offers distance-learning materials to families of adopted children in thirty states, Canada, and England. The center's Chinese Cultural Club provides special activities, such as Chinese games and crafts, to enhance children's knowledge of their native culture, encourage them to form a community of Chinese friends, and instill pride in their heritage.

As adopted children increasingly return to their homeland with their families to pick up a sibling or visit their orphanage, the people of China have been surprised to see Americans with Chinese children who speak English. The curious Chinese who gather around the children delight when a CCAI child can say:

"Ni hao!"

"Wo chu sheng zai Zhong Guo. Wo sheng huo zai Mei Guo."

"I was born in China. I live in America."

LILY ORPHAN CARE CENTERS
Nanny Training and Foster Care

Shou ren yi yu zhu yi ri. Shou ren yi yu zhu yi sheng.
Give a fish to a man and he has food for a day.
Teach a man to fish and he learns a skill for life.

At the turn of the twenty-first century, Lily Orphan Care Centers became a force that helped power dramatic change in China's orphanages, improving the quality of care in facilities where a lack of child-care knowledge caused significant developmental delays in orphans. CCAI worked with China's local governments to open three model orphan care centers, renovating and building orphanages, and hiring and training nannies to demonstrate that institutional care can be high quality and compassionate.

The idea was to provide the best care possible using a child-centered method and to encourage other orphanages to follow CCAI's lead by sending nannies to Lily Orphan Care Centers to receive professional child-care training.

After opening the first center in Hangzhou in Zhejiang Province, CCAI built its next facility in Qidong with a gift from the Essary family. The city in Hunan Province carried special meaning for Linda Essary, a single mom who adopted her first Chinese daughter at the local orphanage, and for Lily, whose mother and father first met in Qidong while serving in Mao's People's Liberation Army.

The third orphan care center was built in the city of Fuling in Chongqing, where hundreds of babies are abandoned each year. Many of the Fuling orphanage children are now placed in foster care through CCAI.

CCAI's philosophy was to build a model facility, train caretakers, and turn over the Lily Orphan Care Center to the local Chinese to run.

In collaboration with China's Ministry of Civil Affairs, CCAI offers child-care training on a national scale. The agency sponsors training conferences each year in designated cities, plus CCAI's child-care team travels throughout China providing on-site training at orphanages. When Lily and Joshua built the first model orphan care center, their dream was to open facilities in every province in China. But as they were preparing to open a fourth facility in 2003, China announced a new policy promoting foster care. The couple immediately shifted gears and started a foster care placement and training program.

"Children belong in homes, not orphanages," said Lily. "Adoption is the final answer for orphans. But before we can find them permanent homes, a temporary home with a mom and dad is a better choice than the best institution."

Joshua's sister, Xia Zhong, who managed the orphan care center in Hangzhou, undertook the tough job of convincing local people who were wary of adoption to become foster parents. After screening and training families to provide quality care, she placed the first fifty orphans sponsored by CCAI and its adoptive families into foster homes in 2003.

CCAI's adoptive families have sponsored thousands of foster children since. By 2009, the agency was sponsoring and supervising eight hundred orphans per year in eleven provinces, and giving hundreds of families who sponsor children quarterly photos and updates on their foster children.

Lily and Joshua launched a new initiative in 2008 to help special-needs orphanage children in the impoverished province of Henan, where 95 percent of orphanage children are physically or mentally impaired. CCAI took over several rooms in the Luo He, Zheng Zhou, and Kai Feng orphanages to create Lily Orphan Care Rooms, providing intensive care and therapy for high-risk children with special needs.

WAITING CHILD PROGRAM

Born with missing fingers and toes and a shortened left leg, Su Gui was a few days old when she was abandoned in Kunming. For her first nine years, she lived in the local orphanage, lonely, hungry, and shunned. A missionary told Lily about the girl, and CCAI placed Su Gui in the home of an American adoptive family. In 2008, at age twenty, Su Gui returned to her homeland to compete on the U.S. Women's Paralympics Volleyball team in the Olympic Games in Beijing. The team won a silver medal.

It was a four-year-old girl named Fang Min who first opened Lily's eyes to what had seemed impossible. At a church service in 1996, a Colorado couple saw a picture of the bowlegged girl standing in the doorway watching American couples pick up their Chinese babies. Something stirred in the hearts of Jeff and Marcia Johnson. Their call to CCAI to find out if they could adopt the child took Lily by surprise. Most families who came to the agency wanted to adopt infants who were healthy. Unsure how officials would respond to the unusual request, Lily called China. Within months CCAI united the Johnsons with their new Chinese daughter.

Five years later, China acknowledged the urgent need to place its huge population of older and special-needs children by creating the Waiting Child Program. Within weeks CCAI opened its own program, taking on a new mission to find homes for children once considered unadoptable. By 2009, the program had placed more than 1,150 older and special-needs children with families.

Lily earlier had embraced the concept that CCAI "leaves no child behind." When a CCAI child was not accepted by a family at match time or in China because of a special need or other reasons, the agency worked to keep track of the orphan, provide financial support to the child, and try to find him or her a new family. Children who could not be placed were provided special care, medical care, and foster care through the Chinese Children Charity Fund.

The Forsleys of Arizona were one of a few CCAI families who left a child behind in China, only to return to adopt the girl they could not forget. The Forsleys knew the second child they were adopting had flat feet, but they had no idea until they met Han Feng, six, that she had trouble walking. At the Hefei hospital in Anhui, they were shocked to learn that Han Feng had a progressive neurological condition that would lead to paralysis and possible death. Devastated, the Forsleys made the heart-wrenching decision to ask for another child. But once home, the torn couple could not stop thinking about the girl back in the orphanage. To their amazement, they saw Han Feng on a television report about the Hefei orphanage and again in a book on China's abandoned children. The Forsleys decided to pay for the girl to have major back surgery in Beijing. They appealed to Lily to help them get Han Feng. By then China had labeled the child unadoptable, and it took six months for Lily to convince the officials to allow the Forsleys to adopt Han Feng. Two years after their first trip to Hefei, the parents were reunited with Han Feng, and they finally brought their third daughter home.

"Adopting an older or special-needs child takes a special family with extra determination, commitment, and love to give," Lily said.

"They are families that have a much bigger love and stronger courage," she said. "They have a spiritual gift to parent special-needs children."

"Most of the time we hear families say, 'This child is meant to be ours. There's a reason she's ours,'" Lily said. "After all these years, you have to believe God's hand is in the whole process."

Two of those special families are the Docters and the Posts, friends who live a mile apart in Michigan. Wendy and Art Docter were raising four biological children in 1996 when they adopted Anye Wu. After the adoption, they discovered their daughter was deaf. Six years later, the Docters agreed to adopt a second deaf girl presented to them by CCAI. In China to get You Ya, they met the girl's three friends, all deaf. You Ya's pictures showed her holding hands with her best friend, You Mei.

Charles and Elaine Post saw the photos and knew You Mei was meant for them. The Posts brought her home on Valentine's Day 2004. When Elaine read a goodbye letter from her new daughter's friend, Chu Zhi Lin, she called CCAI. She learned that in months Zhi Lin and the fourth friend, Yang Shao, would soon turn fourteen, China's cut-off for international adoption.

The Posts and Docters began a race against time. CCAI sped up the process, sending the adoption paperwork to China in record time. A month after the Posts had returned home with You Mei, Elaine and Wendy were in

China adopting the last two friends, just days before one turned fourteen. A year later, all four girls received another miracle — cochlear implants that allowed them to hear for the first time.

Deniece Hess, an adoptive mom of four Chinese girls, including two from the Waiting Child Program, leads a CCAI team that helps bring special-needs children together with new families. These children often face challenges when they come home, struggling to bond with new parents and siblings in a place where they cannot understand or speak the language and must eat food unlike any they've ever tasted. CCAI offers ongoing family support services to adoptive families to help children adjust to a strange new world that can be a frightening place.

ADOPTING HUA GAO JIE

"God had spoken to me: She is yours to love. Take her."
— Joshua Zhong, 2004

For a decade after the birth of Chinese Children Adoption International, Lily and Joshua talked about one day adopting an abandoned Chinese child. The years flew by and the increasing demands of the agency left little time for the founders to focus on their own adoption hopes. The arrival one morning of new files for older and special-needs children awaiting adoption changed all that.

On the table in CCAI's conference room was the information on thirty new children in the Waiting Child Program. The photo on the top of the stack caught Joshua's attention.

"She is so beautiful!" he exclaimed.

"Don't you think she would fit into your family perfectly?" asked Deniece Hess, CCAI's waiting child manager. Joshua glanced up at Lily, who was smiling from across the table.

"She asked me the same question. What do you think?" she asked.

Tentatively, he answered, "Why not?"

Saying nothing more, they returned to their offices. By day's end, the girl's file was on Lily's desk.

She was nine. Born with Tetralogy of Fallot, a severe congenital heart condition, she was four months old when she was abandoned in the ladies restroom in a hospital and delivered to the local child welfare institute in Beijing. In the nation's largest orphanage, the tiny baby was given the name Hua Gao Jie. *Hua* for China, *Gao* for the name of the police station that took her abandonment report, *Jie* for pure.

She was twenty months old when she was taken to the countryside to live with a kind peasant family who raised pigs. The couple provided foster care for three blind, mentally disabled boys. For six years, Gao Jie grew up with foster brothers who could not see or speak. Often she was sick — so sick that she was finally brought back to the city for heart surgery and returned to the orphanage, where she was placed in the Waiting Child Program. Because of her age and heart condition, no one wanted her — until the day Joshua and Lily saw her picture at CCAI.

The following day they flew to Nashville with Amy and Art to attend an adoption conference and CCAI family reunion. At the hotel, Joshua got a call from Dr. Max Mitchell, a pediatric cardiologist at The Children's Hospital in Denver and chair of CCAI's charity fund committee. He had reviewed Gao Jie's medical information and offered to help when the girl was brought home.

That night, Gao Jie's face kept Joshua awake. He closed his eyes to pray. When he opened them, tears were streaming.

"God had spoken to me: 'She is yours to love. Take her.'"

The girl's picture in his hand, Joshua went to his wife and children the next morning.

"What would you think if we brought this nine-year-old girl into our family?" he asked Art and Amy.

"Nine!" said Amy, wide-eyed. She had wanted her parents to adopt a baby but agreed with her mother's wish for a two- or three-year-old.

Amy and Art stared at each other, then at the picture.

"I guess," they both said at once.

Joshua turned to Lily — "Why not?" she said before he could speak. "I was just waiting on all of you."

The frustrating paper chase and the anxious wait for their daughter gave Lily and Joshua a new perspective on the adoption process.

"It gave us a new understanding about the struggle, excitement, and jubilation of our adoptive families," Lily said.

On October 25, 2004, Lily and Joshua joined the adoptive families they had for so long served. In the Beijing orphanage, they held their new daughter for the first time. They named the smiling girl with pigtails Anna Jie Zhong. They also gave her a new Chinese name, Qing, which means love. Together with Art and Amy's Chinese names, it means "love for China."

At home, the new member of the family surprised her brother and sister by hand-washing her own dirty socks and hanging them up to dry. A few weeks later, Anna, who like her mother came to America speaking no English, enrolled in elementary school.

Adopting Anna also brought home the challenges faced by parents who adopt older and special-needs children and the need to prepare for behaviors related to orphanage life. At school, Anna struggled to keep up with her lessons. At home, she had to learn not to lie, hoard food, or mistreat her toys.

A few years after Anna settled into her new life in America, a family friend delivered a letter from the girl's foster mother, who wrote:

"I received the photos you sent. … I see an innocent and lively little Gao Jie again … Having homes in both the United States and China, you are the luckiest child in the world."

Lily and Joshua believe they are the lucky ones. They are certain that they were meant to adopt Anna.

"We thank God for his wonderful gift of life and love," Joshua said. "We are truly blessed."

RED THREAD COUNSELING CENTER
ChinaRoots and AdopTeen Conference

After more than five thousand child placements, a CCAI survey in 2005 on the needs of its adoptive families showed that some were struggling with orphanage-related behaviors, attachment, bonding, or other adoption issues. That was enough to convince Lily and Joshua to open a China adoption counseling center to support its families.

The children in the earliest groups who had arrived in the U.S. in 1994 were becoming adolescents, a time when struggles with emotional and identity issues often begin. Some other families whose adopted children had been home from eighteen months to four years were experiencing behavioral issues. Many of the adoptive families were first-time parents in their forties, and some were questioning their own parenting skills.

Recognizing the need for counseling and consultation services for families facing the unique history and experiences of orphanage children, Lily and Joshua opened the Red Thread Counseling Center. The name comes from an ancient Chinese belief that says when a child is born she is connected to the most important people in her life — even those she is destined to meet but has not yet met — by an unbreakable red thread.

The counseling center offers the services of professional counselors with clinical skills and experience in mental health, adoption, and attachment issues. It is a place for families to go for support, therapy, and consultation for issues related to adoption, growth, and family dynamics. The counselors offer play therapy for children, family therapy, phone consultation for parents, and therapy for issues related to attachment problems, trauma, grief, and loss. They coach parents on how to determine what is normal behavior for a certain growth stage and what is adoption- or trauma-related. If unable to provide the help a family needs, the center offers referrals to other qualified professionals.

"Infants are completely dependent on a caring person to meet their every need, twenty-four hours a day. This is how they develop a deep sense of trust and security as well as an ability to regulate their emotions," said Janelle Althen, Red Thread director. "Even in the best orphanages, the caregiver-to-child ratio makes it difficult for children to get what they need, which can impact their emotional development in subtle or overt ways."

Adopted Chinese children have experienced the neurological and emotional trauma of loss, neglect, and repeated transitions. They first lose their biological mothers when they're abandoned, sometimes waiting alone for hours to be found. Next they live in an orphanage with dozens of other orphans. Often they're placed with foster parents until they're matched with an American family — only to return to the orphanage again before being adopted. Finally, they're taken to live with a new family in a strange new country.

"Infants are designed to be cared for in a home day and night by their mothers in a one-on-one relationship," said Janelle. "It's traumatic to their systems not to have that connection."

In addition to working with parents on behavioral issues, the Red Thread center also counsels families on how to help their children integrate all facets of their identity — Chinese, American, adopted — in a healthy way.

"We want to help parents maximize their abilities to become healing agents in their children's lives," Janelle said.

To facilitate a part of that healing process, CCAI created its ChinaRoots program in 2006 offering pilgrimages back to China for adoptive families. Unlike traditional tours, ChinaRoots arranges return visits to adoptive children's abandonment sites, orphanages, and foster homes, along with opportunities for families to immerse themselves in the local culture and traditions.

To meet the needs of CCAI children who are now teens, the agency sponsored the first annual AdopTeen Conference in 2008. Teens from around the nation gathered at CCAI to bond over the adoption and identity issues they face as they write the history of the first wave of adopted Chinese children to call America home. Amy and Art Zhong have taken leading roles in planning the event and working with the teens.

CCAI ADOPTIONS, BY YEAR

1994 20	2002 739	2010 580
1995 140	2003 781	2011 479
1996 282	2004 952	2012 478
1997 210	2005 1,152	2013 472
1998 467	2006 767	2014 484
1999 424	2007 613	
2000 626	2008 422	TOTAL
2001 600	2009 443	11,131

HONORS

2003
Congressional Angels in Adoption Award: Lily Nie and Joshua Zhong
Rotary Club Centennial Four – Way Test Award: Joshua Zhong

2004
The Sixth Annual Colorado Chinese Model Mother's Award: Lily Nie

2006
Colorado Parents of the Year: Joshua Zhong and Lily Nie

2008
Colorado Women's Hall of Fame: Lily Nie

2010
Women Who Change the Heart of City from Denver Rescue Mission:
    Lily Nie

2011
#1 Ranked China Adoption Agency in the World for Overall Services:
    CCAI

2012
Community Service Award from University of Phoenix: Lily Nie

2013
Be More Award for Innovative Leadership from Rocky Mountain PBS:
    Lily Nie

AUTHOR'S NOTE

My daughter is one of the thousands of Chinese children Lily Nie has saved. In 1995, the year Lily first started rescuing babies from the orphanage warfront, I was forty-two and single, trying to reconcile to the real probability that I would never be a mother. On an otherwise ordinary day, I read a story in the *Rocky Mountain News,* where I was an editor, announcing the arrival of the first wave of Chinese orphans brought to Colorado by Chinese Children Adoption International. That Thanksgiving, I stood in a Hangzhou hotel in the province of Zhejiang, holding my new daughter in my arms.

She was four months and weighed just eight and a half pounds. Ni Feng, whose name became Neely Anna, and eight other babies in Group Sixteen were delivered into our lives with almost no information. I wondered how on earth this tiny black-haired baby had been matched to me, half a world away.

"God is the matchmaker," CCAI's representative in China told me solemnly.

Always I have answered my daughter's questions surrounding her humble beginnings by telling her the truth from what very little I knew. What I came to believe I could do for my daughter, and for the other abandoned children rescued from China's orphanages by Lily Nie, was to tell them the love story of the woman who changed fate by answering the call to do the matchmaker's work.

— Linda Droeger is a former editor of the *Rocky Mountain News, Denver Post, Chicago Tribune,* and *Atlanta Constitution.* She lives in a suburb of Denver, Colorado, with her daughter.

ACKNOWLEDGMENTS

The families of adopted Chinese children helped me write *Bound by Love*. Their memories and those of Lily Nie and Joshua Zhong, their devoted staff, families, and mentors are knitted into the story of how individuals come together to change the world.

Thank you to those who openly shared their hearts and their stories with me. I am deeply grateful to my family and friends for all of their support during the researching and writing of this book. *Bound by Love* came to life with the encouragement of many caring people, including adoptive parents Barbara and Jonathan Slaton, and the skill of editor Brian Schoeni and his wife, Megan, adoptive parents, and author Patricia Raybon. I am grateful to them all and to the thousands of children whose lives helped shape this story, including my daughter, Neely, and her adopted Chinese cousins, Tao Zhu and Quinn; Art, Amy, and Anna Zhong; and Malena, Corinne, and Lucinda.

Our deepest appreciation to renowned illustrator Mary GrandPré, mother of a daughter adopted through CCAI, who created the beautiful cover for *Bound by Love*. We also are very grateful to Meriwether Publishing's Mark Zapel, father of an adopted Chinese daughter, who diligently oversaw the publication of this book.

Most of all, thank you to China for entrusting its children to us. We are deeply grateful to our children's homeland for recognizing the crisis in its child welfare institutes and opening the doors to adoption by foreigners to find homes for abandoned children. Thanks to the orphanages that invested the child-rearing fees received over the last fifteen years into improving orphanage conditions and to those caretakers who worked endless hours to save the lives of our children in a painfully difficult time.

My sincere appreciation to all the people whose stories appear in *Bound by Love*, including:

- The parents of Lily, Liu Liang Zhen and Nie Guang Qian; and Joshua, Zhong Wang Kun and the late Zhong Wei Quan.
- Mentors, Dr. Jack and Liz Layman, and Dr. Ralph and the late Ruth Covell.
- Adoptive families, including Chuck and Eileen Berling, David and Janet Schroeder, Jim and Tish Joros, Joan Ditges, Darrell and Patti Doering, Dr. David and Rebecca Blank, Tom Ponrick and Leslie Ponrick.
- Chinese Children Adoption International's dedicated current and former workers and volunteers in the United States and China, including Victoria and Chris Lierheimer, Kat LaMons, Katie Faust, Deniece Hess, Xia Zhong, Gu Jian Ping, Ken Zhu, Thomas He and Raymond Xiang.
- Guiding lights Kit Ying Chang of Mother's Love and Dr. Liu Xiang Guo of the Changsha Children's Hospital.

— Linda Droeger

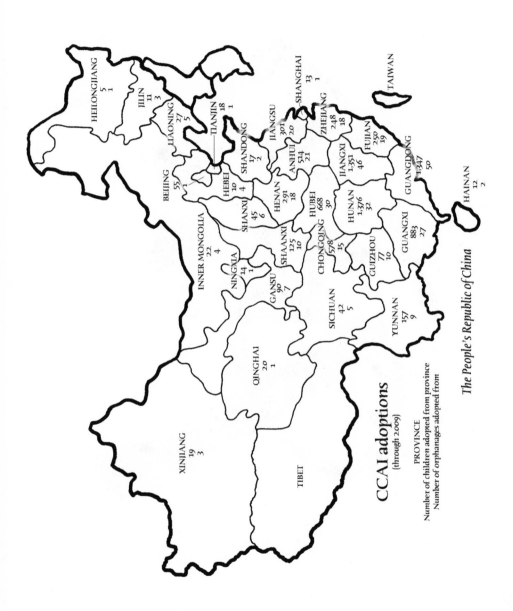

CCAI adoptions
(through 2009)

PROVINCE
Number of children adopted from province
Number of orphanages adopted from

The People's Republic of China

HEILONGJIANG
5
1

JILIN
11
3

LIAONING
27
5

TIANJIN
18
1

BEIJING
55

SHANDONG
17
2

JIANGSU
301
20

SHANGHAI
13
1

ZHEJIANG
18

HEBEI
10
4

SHANXI
45
6

HENAN
291
18

ANHUI
534
21

JIANGXI
1,351
46

FUJIAN
250
19

GUANGDONG
1,347
50

TAIWAN

HUBEI
668
30

HUNAN
1,376
32

GUANGXI
883
27

HAINAN
12
2

INNER MONGOLIA
22
4

SHAANXI
125
10

CHONGQING
578
15

GUIZHOU
77
10

NINGXIA
14
1

GANSU
90
7

SICHUAN
42
5

YUNNAN
157
9

QINGHAI
20
1

XINJIANG
19
3

TIBET